WHOLE PERSON
HAPPINESS

HOW TO BE WELL IN BODY, MIND & SPIRIT

Paul Krismer, B.A., C.E.C.
"The Happiness Expert"

Publication Date: 2017

©2017 by Paul Krismer. All Rights Reserved.

Edited by: Carmel Ecker, Speak Now Communications

Design, Layout and Graphics by: Carmel Ecker, Speak Now Communications

ISBN-10:154537113X

ISBN-13:9781545371138

This book is based on the personal experience and opinions of the author. Note that the advice provided herein does not substitute for competent financial, medical, and/or psychological advice that you may receive, or may be advisable to receive, from a licensed practitioner. The author will not be held liable or responsible to any person or entity with respect to alleged damaged caused directly or indirectly by the information within this book.

In some instances, names and places have been changed to protect the identity of those involved.

Paul Krismer

Paul@HappinessExperts.ca

www.HappinessExperts.ca

CONTENTS

Introduction 1

Chapter 1: How to Approach Happiness 7

Chapter 2: The Whole Person 15

PART ONE: BODY – PHYSICAL WELL-BEING   27

Chapter 3: Fitness 29

Chapter 4: Nutrition.. 37

Chapter 5: Sleep, Rest and Sex 49

Chapter 6: Disease and Aging... 59

Chapter 7: Money 65

Chapter 8: Safety and Security.. 71

PART TWO: MIND – MENTAL AND EMOTIONAL HAPPINESS   79

Chapter 9: Continuous Learning... 81

Chapter 10: Discipline and Ambition.. 89

Chapter 11: Creativity and Curiosity 99

Chapter 12: Critical Thinking... 103

Chapter 13: Love.. 113

Chapter 14: Friends and Community... 121

Chapter 15: Belonging to Your Tribe 127

Chapter 16: Culture Connects Us.. 133

PART THREE: SPIRIT   139

Chapter 17: Contemplation and Mindfulness 143

Chapter 18: Contemplative Connection... 155

Chapter 19: Gratitude 161

Chapter 20: Cultivation of Quality Character 167

Summary 173

Afterword 179

Acknowledgements 181

INTRODUCTION

I took my first paper route when I was eight years old. I was a very little person—barely four feet tall—and life was a game full of wonder and endless play. I suppose money was a motivator, but I think it was largely also a matter of having something to do. I wasn't busy after school, which is when this daily paper needed to be delivered. It was simply "normal" that I should take the route when it was offered. The paper route was small—I could do the whole circuit in about a half hour. And on most weekdays, the paper was relatively thin so it was an easy load to carry in a satchel hung over my shoulder.

Once a week, I had to collect the newspaper subscription fee. Nearly 40 years later, I can still vividly recall the fun I had at special customers' houses. One gentleman loved to pretend he was paying with counterfeit money—I always laughed and vaguely wondered if it truly was funny money. A kindly old couple, whose house smelled of medicinal mint, always let me take one wrapped candy out of a special crystal bowl. After several years of the same routine, I came to realize the bowl was always well stocked with my favorite, a hard caramel wrapped in shiny red foil.

On many occasions, my cat would follow me around the route that began and ended at my home. King Kong Kitty Cat Krismer, as the neighbors called our large feline, would play this game where he would pretend he wasn't following me. If I looked back at him, he would turn away and start walking in a new direction. A minute later I would sneak another look and almost always he was back on my trail. I fondly recall how my cat, like me, was very proper and kept to the sidewalks, rarely cutting across someone's front lawn.

I remember that, in the autumn, I would sometimes get so distracted playing in all the fallen leaves that it would take me 2 hours to do my 30 minute route. The air was fresh and I felt alive. I didn't consciously know it then, but I was thoroughly enjoying the exercise.

After I paid my paper's distributor his cut of the paper route money, I was always thrilled with my little stash of cash (mostly coins actually). Typically, on Friday afternoon after the route was complete, I would go to the corner store a couple of blocks away with my best friend, who also had a paper route. We would buy penny candy and sometimes a bit of butcher's bacon. We were proud entrepreneurs relishing the fruit of our labor.

I kept on delivering newspapers for six years—six days a week, with progressively larger routes. Delivering newspapers made me happy. It was rewarding to walk up to the front door and leave this product that people wanted.

Now many years later, I understand why the act of delivering newspapers made me happy. Through my work as a professional life coach and years of personal research on the subject of happiness, I've learned that happiness relies on us fulfilling a core set of needs. These needs are the same for everyone. It's how we fill them that varies. Every client I've worked with, regardless of their reasons for hiring me, has wanted simply to be happy. They rarely state their interest as plainly as that, but at the root of all yearning is the desire for happiness. Even in my role as a Certified Executive Coach, helping powerful decision-makers become better leaders, I am helping clients find greater meaning, fulfillment and pleasure in their life. I hope this book does the same for you.

Are you happy right now? Do you have a big, giddy grin on your face? Probably not. Nevertheless, you may feel content. You are likely someplace warm and comfortable, enjoying the process of your eyes scanning the page as each sentence triggers stimulating thoughts in your brain. Perhaps you have already lost your focus on my written words and momentarily broken away into your imagination or your own memories of childhood. Maybe you have a sense of hope for the future and you have picked up this book with a quest for a new beginning and an earnest searching

Happiness relies on us fulfilling a core set of needs.

for a happier you. All of these perspectives may fall within a broad concept of happiness.

The emotion we call happiness is multi-faceted. It includes the obvious: moments of cheerfulness such as enjoying a big belly laugh with a good friend or receiving a gift you really like. It also includes the contentment you feel when you have accomplished a challenging task, such as a project at work or a crossword puzzle. Happiness is also the satisfaction and pleasure of enjoying your own company—perhaps reading a book or daydreaming while you look out your living room window. This broad view of the qualities of life that make us feel good is the subject of the first chapter of this book. Within this chapter, you will discover that the quest for happiness has rich avenues of discovery and mastery.

We explore the concept of the whole person in Chapter Two. Happiness can't be found in just one area of our lives. We all know this intuitively, but sometimes people get lost hoping to find soul satisfaction in one place. The addict is an extreme example of this. He craves for the one and only thing that makes him happy, or at least makes him feel less pain. Life becomes reduced to the pursuit of the one thing he can equate with happiness. We all know other types of short-sighted behaviors. Do you know anyone who serves others to the point that they become victims of their own selflessness? They have become doormats to the homes of other people's happiness. This trait is rooted in a time when that person found satisfaction in helping others—as we all do—but they lost the balance required in their lives. Their own personal happiness has been sacrificed as they pursue a singular, unbalanced attempt at soul satisfaction. Chapter Two explains in detail how we are all made up of three essential domains: body, mind (emotional and mental) and spirit. Each of these domains must have its needs met in order for us to grow to be happy people in the long run.

Once there is a clear understanding of the whole person concept, we are ready for the journey to begin. We are ready to explore the landscape that makes up each of our three essential domains: body, mind and spirit. Each of these three domains warrants its own section in this book:

- Part One focuses on Body, examining our physical selves.

- Part Two examines Mind, including both mental stimulation and emotional well-being.

- Part Three is about Spirit, exploring our connection to all people, nature and our own consciousness. This domain is not about religion. If you have a particular religious doctrine that is meaningful to you, you may find your spirituality within the context of that doctrine. Yet, if you don't find any particular religious doctrine meaningful, you can still fully embrace and enjoy the spiritual life described in this section of the book.

You may already be quite happy in one or more of these domains. Most of my coaching clients have a high level of contentment in some areas of their life so we don't methodically develop actions plans for each domain. We work together to see where strengths already exist and then grow them and cheerily exploit them. Next, we determine what area of their life needs attention. Together, we hone in on the area of interest—something they yearn for—that gives that specific client energy. To be successful, the client needs to get excited to take action and he or she must know there is a worthy destination on the road ahead.

If you have mastered any of the domains of body, mind or spirit, congratulations! You are well begun on your journey. In that case, parts of this book may be less relevant for you. You may choose to skim over or skip altogether the chapter on nutrition if you are already a culinary master of healthy eating. If you have a life full of encouraging friends and family, you may find less need to consider the chapter on relationships. The value in this book will be found in deep reflection on the sections where you have not yet cultivated mastery. If you know your spiritual life is as dry as the Sahara Desert then slow down when you are reading Part Three. Take lots of notes and determine a realistic action plan for you to begin winning back your right to this source of happiness.

We all need to start small. Henry Ford, the inventor of the industrial assembly line observed, "Nothing is particularly hard if you divide it into small jobs." With this belief, Ford went on to build millions of extraordinarily complex machines and one of the world's most successful businesses. Our own growth should be similar. We are not expected to take all the missing pieces of our lives and assemble them all at once. Instead, focus most intently on one or two small things. I suggest you start with goals that are not too large a stretch. If physical fitness is an area of weakness, don't begin by committing to create a body builder's physique or a marathon runner's stamina. Start with modest, attainable goals in one small area: "I will walk up the stairs at work rather than take the elevator". Whatever your goal is, begin slowly. But begin.

You are ready to begin your journey of discovery and increased joy. The pages

ahead are intended as a blessing to your life. Savor the learning. I encourage you to have a note pad with you or to write generously in the margins of the pages. Research shows note-taking is a powerful aid to learning. Mark down what strikes you as most important or what your priorities for self development reveal themselves to be.

Your happy self wants you to come and find him or her. Read on so you know where to look.

Begin . . . begin . . . begin!

1 How to Approach Happiness

Plato, the great Greek philosopher, had a theory that can entirely change your life. He had a Theory of Forms. He believed that what we think about a subject is the closest to the truth of the matter; in other words, our conceptual understanding of something is more true than what our sensory experience informs us.

To illustrate, let's consider the example Plato gave: the idea of a triangle. In our minds, we can conjure up the image of a perfect triangle. We can define its qualities, such as all its interior angles add up to exactly 180 degrees, the lines along its sides are perfectly straight, and there are three connected sides. I could express this thought of a triangle and most people could agree on the "idea" of a perfect triangle.

We may set out to build a triangle so we can experience the shape with our physical senses. Perhaps we find three sticks in the forest and lay them down in the shape of a triangle. Would it be perfect? No. It would have flaws. The sticks would have bumps and indentations so the lines of our triangle wouldn't be perfectly straight. Also, the interior angles wouldn't likely add up to exactly 180 degrees. Our idea of a perfect triangle would be at odds with our imperfect construction of a triangle. And this difference will always be true no matter how carefully and precisely we build one out of physical materials. Even if we use beautifully milled lumber rather than sticks, a careful analysis will find flaws. Even if we had engineers design and construct their best triangle out of metal pieces with precision tools, we would always find room for improvement. As our methods of construction improve, so too do our mechanisms for measurement. All physical triangles will be imperfect by some measure. And so it is with our lives.

Plato's theory of forms applies in a practical way to each of us. We can each conceive of the perfect person we are. In our minds, we can be very clear about our own ideal form. I can imagine what my perfect physical health looks and feels like. I can also envision my best spiritual or intellectual self. The reality is that I won't likely live up to those visions. This is Plato's theory at work—perfection, or ideal forms, exist in our minds. The physical (or real world) manifestations of these ideals fall short of what we imagined.

Contrary to what you might believe, this is good!

By considering the ideal form in each of our domains, we become much clearer about our goals. We construct a mental map of where we want to be in relation to where we are now. Plato's Theory of Forms explains that perfection is an imaginary thing, worthy of our reflection, but not achievable in the world of our tangible (sensory) experience.

This book describes some ideals for each of our domains, but doesn't prescribe that we somehow achieve the ideal physical, mental, emotional or spiritual outcomes. Instead, by conceiving where we want to go—that is, by describing the destination—we become clearer about our road map to get there. This book lets you off the hook from any pressure to be perfect. I want each reader to find increased happiness and health in their physical, mental, emotional and spiritual lives. There is, however, no perfect place for you to have pure bliss all the time. We get to be human—fallible and flawed. From that realistic starting place, we can seek out and move toward our best experience of happiness and health. I fully admit my state of non-perfection. I get sick infrequently, but it does happen. I am sometimes mentally lazy. My social life has occasional conflict. And, alas, my spiritual journey has been known to take me down dark, dead-end roads. BUT, for every dead end I have found myself in, I believe that by having a picture of perfection in my mind I have been able to recognize when I was stuck and reset my direction back toward my destination.

I hope this book will guide you like a map. Where you feel disoriented or directionless in one or more of your domains, use this book to determine the right direction.

When I was a boy, delivering newspapers was a tremendously positive experience. It was not perfect. Some days were brutally cold and I dreaded the task. Near Christmas, when the advertising flyers stuffed the newspapers to three and four times their normal size, I struggled to carry them all. Occasionally, I resented the responsibility because I couldn't linger at school and play with my friends. There were drawbacks—imperfections—in my endeavor.

> I spent time alone being reflective and enjoying the fresh air and beauty of nature.

Yet the lesson of the paper route was, on the whole, overwhelmingly positive. It kept me fit while I earned money. I learned responsibility, money management, and the importance of devising a plan and then executing it. I got to know the families and characters of the majority of my neighborhood. And I spent time alone being reflective and enjoying the fresh air and beauty of nature. My paper route is an analogy for life. Come with me as we deliver the news! Let's explore ways to make life more fulfilling.

A Brief Primer on Positive Psychology

We are so lucky to be alive at this time. The field of positive psychology has exploded into mainstream research. Expert knowledge about being happy can be found in any good book store. This knowledge makes my job as a coach so much easier. I am profoundly grateful for the help found in many books and articles written for the general public.

For the rest of this chapter I will lay out a few of the most basic findings about happiness and well-being that have been discovered and verified through rigorous scientific research. Modern science has much to tell us about what makes us feel good. Hundreds of studies have been done using controlled, repeatable experiments to see how subjects react to stimuli and which stimuli have the biggest and longest lasting beneficial effects. As well, neuropsychology has fundamentally changed the way we understand the brain and our emotions.

Three Parts of the Brain

Human beings are extraordinary products of millions of years of evolution. Our ancestors include single-cell organisms that floated in ancient seas. With the passage of time our predecessors grew appendages and crawled out of the water onto land. After the age of dinosaurs, mammals became prominent. From there, primates evolved with sophisticated thinking. Fast-forward a million years and here we are—the most advanced brain owners in the known universe.

Our large and complex brains are so fantastic mostly because of the ability to think. We do this better than any other animal. But we also have rich information contained in our emotions, which is common to mammals generally. And, of course, we have automatic systems that manage breathing, digesting food and all manner of basic physical processes.

As humans evolved from other life forms, we built onto the architecture of more primitive brains, adding progressively more complex and dynamic neural structures. We essentially have three brain components that seamlessly interact with one another: reptile, mammal and primate.

At the low centre of our skulls, we have a brain that manages automatic and essential biological functions like breathing, digesting food, moving blood around our bodies, etc. This is our reptilian brain. Simplistically, we could say it's about our bodies. It manages the functions required for survival. This brain automatically provides physical reactions to any perceived threat.

The part of our brain that's above and around our reptilian brain is the one that provides emotional rewards. This is our mammalian brain. This area generally motivates us to move towards that which we desire. It makes us feel good when we eat a tasty meal, slip into a warm bath or watch a heart-warming movie. It's our "feeling" emotional brain.

Our large cerebral cortex at the top and front of our skull is the primate brain. It does our thinking. It manages and analyzes both emotional and sensory input. It has evolved largely to help us manage the complex social environments that humans (and many other primates) live in. This means that our reasoning brain exists, in some significant part, to help us form secure relationships with other people.

For us to be happy and content, all three brains need to have their specific needs met. We need to:

- ensure our reptilian needs for physical wellness are met.

- satisfy mammalian needs of contentment and emotional rewards.

- engage our thinking brains with novel stimulation, and secure meaningful attachments with others.

We can weave a thread of well-being through all three brains when we deliberately work to create greater harmony amongst them.

Reptile-brain needs: food, shelter, sleep and overall physical security. When these are absent, happiness is difficult to experience. If we're hungry or exhausted, we can't pursue pleasures in other areas of life. If there is a threat to our physical security (or a perceived one), then we can't relax and enjoy companionship, reflection or intellectual engagement. These physical needs are primary. They tend to be most compelling in their absence. When they are met, however, other physical needs can be sought after. Sex, nice clothes, music and all manner of sensory pleasures contribute to the experience of well-being. When physical needs are satisfied, we are relaxed and can move toward meeting the needs of our other two brains.

Mammal-brain needs: comfort found in food, a peaceful hike in the woods, time with family or any other experiences that give rise to positive emotions. These allow our brains to release positive hormones throughout our bodies. When these needs are met, we are content; we see the world as a good place that provides for us. When our emotions are generally content, then our stress is lowered, we have greater resilience, and opportunity to explore our own strengths and interests.

Primate-brain needs: mental stimulation and attachment; that is, a deep sense of belonging. Our brains have considerable architecture devoted to reading and understanding other people's emotions. We use empathy to make important social connections. When these needs are ideally met, we are curious and playful. We have at least a few social connections that give us profound meaning, security and joy—we are loved and loving. Fortunately, our primate brain allows us to use reason and self-directed behavior to enhance our ability to meet our own needs.

This simplistic explanation of the three brains will be useful as you consider how you can enhance your life. You can't satisfy the needs of just one or two of your brains; rather, you must broadly consider all three regions of the brain and the interplay between them.

Happiness Defined

There are many ways to look at of the idea of happiness. I've touched on several already. In spiritual terms, happiness is a sense of inner peace. There is no greater satisfaction than to be content regardless of the circumstances you find yourself in. Feelings of universal love, forgiveness, and acceptance of "what is" are all founda-

tions of inner peace. This may, however, feel a bit esoteric, so let's consider the way scientists define happiness. My favorite approach is that of Barbara Fredrickson.

Fredrickson is a psychology professor at the University of North Carolina. Arguably, she is one of the foremost scholars on the topic of positive emotions. She defines happiness as the presence of one or more of the following positive emotions: joy, gratitude, serenity, interest, hope, pride, amusement, inspiration, awe and love. When we are experiencing any one of these feelings, we are happy. I appreciate her practical and understandable framing of the idea of happiness. It allows us to get real about when we feel good. Take a moment to consider each of these distinct feelings.

Joy — Imagine a time when you were clearly delighted with a positive event that was realized in your life. Perhaps you won a prize, earned a bonus at work or enjoyed a good laugh with friends. Pause for a moment and consider when you had a clearly delightful moment. Feel joy.

Gratitude — Recall when someone did something unexpected, generous and of genuine assistance to you. It could be a simple gesture, such as your neighbor scraping the frost off your windshield, another driver allowing you to merge in busy traffic or your friend cheerfully lending a hand with a yard project. Pause and think of a time when an act of kindness made your life a bit more pleasant. Feel gratitude.

Serenity — Consider a moment when you felt relaxed, peaceful and comfortable, like standing next to a warm fire on an autumn day. Maybe on a hike, you were amazed by a beautiful scene—a rushing waterfall, a gentle brook dappled with sunshine, a gorgeous sunset as the sun disappeared behind the mountains. If you're a home body, you could feel serenity while snuggled on the couch with a cup of hot tea and a beautiful piece of music playing in the background. Consider a past experience of serenity. Feel it.

Interest — When have you felt a deep sense of interest in something? Perhaps you listened to a fascinating speaker, learned a new skill or discovered a new and better way to approach a familiar task. Remember what that felt like to be engaged and have the opportunity to explore.

Hope — Hope arises when current circumstances are undesirable, yet you can sense there is a way out. You might feel this when you are struggling with a work task, but begin to sense a way forward, or when you end a relationship, but have a reservoir of confidence that, in spite of the pain, you now have time and opportunity to get to know other people. Hope motivates action. Stir the sense of hope.

Pride — There can be swollen, inappropriate and unhelpful pride, but at this moment consider only genuine and kind-hearted pride. When you are being good and honest with yourself, you see your best qualities. Consider a time when you felt good about yourself. Perhaps you performed well at work or you stopped to help someone who dropped her bag or you finished painting a room in your house and were happy with the results. Focus on a time when you felt healthy, well-earned pride.

Amusement — Amusement is generally spontaneous and out of the ordinary. You are caught off guard, but not in a threatening way. You feel alive and have heightened mood when you share a laugh over a funny experience. This feeling arises when a co-worker makes a witty observation, a frog unexpectedly hops in front of you and a friend while on a walk, or your 4-year-old accidentally tries to pull a shirt over his head through the sleeve. Bring to mind a time when you were amused. Feel the levity and pleasantness of the experience.

Inspiration — When humanity, in some form or fashion, rises above its usual experience and does something truly amazing, we are inspired. Imagine a time when you saw an act of great compassion. It could be scenes on the news following a natural disaster when ordinary people tried to rescue and tend to the wounds of strangers. Or an artist revealed a work so exquisite that it made you see the world in a different light. Summon that feeling in your mind.

Awe — Awe is powerful and bigger than one's ordinary life circumstances. You experience it when you witness something that stops you in your tracks. Sights such as the Grand Canyon or the Egyptian pyramids inspire awe with their magnitude. Human firsts such as the moon landing and seemingly impossible challenges such as a mother protecting her children from a bear can leave our mouths agape. Awe is an experience of mental transcendence where you are instantly carried away from usual states of mind and experience something that generally defies expression in words. Visualize something that has caused you to be blown away.

Love — Love is the experience of one or more of the previously described emotions felt in the context of a personal relationship. It's a separate and yet inclusive positive emotion. If you are a parent, recall when your first child took his or her first step. You likely experienced interest, hope, awe, gratitude and pride all at once. Remember when a good friend graduated from school and was overwhelmed with the relief and pleasure in her accomplishment. You empathetically shared her emotions because your love gave rise to the experience of her accomplishment being a source of your own happiness. Love is an especially powerful form of positive emotion. Bring to mind your feelings of love for someone close to you: your parent, your son or daughter, or a life partner.

I'm grateful for the grounding these 10 positive emotions give to the meaning of happiness. When we think about each of these feelings, we know they are what make life rich and beautiful. Joy, gratitude, serenity, interest, hope, pride, amusement, inspiration, awe and love are what we all want. This book can help you open pathways to these positive feelings. Harmonious lives with a balanced foundation in all three domains—body, mind and spirit—give rise to many positive emotions.

2 The Whole Person

Imagine a writer engaged in her task. As she taps keys and looks at a monitor, her mind generates ideas and expresses the ideas in language. The language magically appears in the form of symbols arranged in precise order on a screen. She is calm, yet she has a certain intensity—her interest is piqued. She intends for her creation to uplift and reach readers in some place of an unmet need. The writer's whole person is engaged in the task harmoniously; that is, no part of her is rebelling or disharmonious. Her whole person is tracking well. Let me explain how this writer can have complete congruence in the moment: body, mind and spirit.

Physically, she has no need that is overwhelming or crying out for attention. Let's assume it is not quite 6:00 a.m. Our writer has slept solidly. She feels fresh. Her home and neighborhood are quiet. She will soon need to eat but presently she is content. With no thought or worry, she breathes. With no effort or conscious awareness her eyes and hands work together to take the words that come to her mind and physically produce these thoughts on her computer. She is sitting comfortably with very little awareness of any physical need. Her body is in harmony with the activity. It's an active partner in the writing, but it is not the driver of the activity.

Our writer's body will sustain this activity for a reasonably long period, but at some point disharmony could result if she ignores her physical needs. She will get hungry, for example. As this need for nutrition grows more compelling, her presently quiet reptilian brain—that most primitive, earliest evolved part of our brain—will become demanding and force its agenda onto her thinking brain. She may choose to ignore hunger for a while, but her hunger will become overwhelmingly disharmonious with continued writing activity. It will demand attention in her cerebral cortex—the most recently evolved, thinking part of our brain. And she will become grumpy and discontent with her activity (dampening the experience of the mammalian brain). The need for food will cause her stomach to rumble, her hand-eye coordination to diminish, her feelings to become upset and her thinking to become distracted to the point of being unable to effectively stay on track. The task switches from writing to the pursuit of food.

She is a writer. She is also a body that needs food. And indeed, she is also a social creature; a daughter, a friend and family member. She may or may not have harmonious contentment—a congruency within the multiple domains of her whole being: body, mind, and spirit.

Connectivity of the Domains

I am my body but I am not just my body. I am a social animal but I am not just a social being. I am a thinker who undertakes deliberate mental processes, but I am much more than my mind. And I am someone who connects with others and my world in a spiritual way, but I am by no means just a soul pursuing my notion of "god".

Then what am I?

Humans are beautifully complex individuals who inhabit multiple spaces at the same time. I have referred to these spaces as domains. We have three of them: body, mind and spirit. Let's imagine these domains as separate spaces for a moment. Our planet consists of different ecosystems. Nature is in balance in the presence of different, distinct spaces. In ancient times, nature was assigned to four simple elements: earth, water, fire and air.

Earth consists of rocks and dirt. Rocks and dirt have their own place. We don't see these in the air or occupying the spaces where water is predominant. Similarly, water mostly has its own spaces, distinct from where air or earth predominate. Each of these elements has its own character. For example, air is in circulation; it is lightweight, transparent and serves the planet through the provision of oxygen and carbon dioxide.

Each element is distinct from the other. However, we know that these four elements are interconnected components that make up our planet. At many levels they are intermingled, dependent on one another and even made up of one

another. For example, water is constantly permeating earth, evaporating to air, and condensing and precipitating back to earth. Our planet is alive with all manner of creatures and plants that are made up of water, air and minerals from the earth.

On our living planet it's difficult to distinguish where one element begins and another ends. At the seashore, where does the water's edge meet the earth? The tide constantly blurs the line. And the earth does not come to the water's edge and cease, but carries on to become the ocean floor. As water washes over land, it erodes rock and pulls the loose earth into the ocean, lake or stream. So the earth is present in the water.

This is also the nature of our three human domains. My physical body is distinct and separate from my mental and emotional states. Physically, I have specific character traits—tall and thin, healthy blood pressure, and so on. Socially, I am a bit shy, passionate, curious... Similarly, my mental character is its own thing: bright, verbal, poor at spatial geometry... Spiritually, I am seeking, appreciative and have a tendency to doubt...

Each of my three domains—body, mind and spirit—has its own characteristics. Like earth, water and air, however, the domains of my personhood are inextricably linked and commingled. This is more true than most of us realize. For example, we can't be physically well if we are emotionally unwell. The marathon runner who has chronic marriage issues will not only suffer the emotional pain associated with a broken relationship, but she will also inevitably underperform on the track. The stress from her social life constantly fills her body with hormonal surges intended to combat adversity. So when she is recovering from a long run, her body is also coping with massive hormonal floods in the bloodstream that require their own healing. If the relationship issues persist, the body is constantly in a state of stress. The energy that could be devoted to improving lung capacity and muscle growth is re-directed—at least in part—to managing the damage caused by chronic stress. This is not to suggest that the runner isn't benefiting from her exercise. Indeed, the exercise is likely helping her cope with stress; however, she can't maximize her physical health under the circumstances.

The interdependency of each domain is unavoidable. Our unfortunate runner can't be her best physically unless she recovers emotionally. Similarly, a man who has a terrific social life, but is chronically physically unwell, will inevitably experience diminished social well-being. For example, if he is overweight, he will become out of breath with minor physical activity. His social character will suffer when he cannot carry on a conversation because the act of climbing a single set of stairs leaves him momentarily gasping for breath.

Our whole person—all three domains—must be healthy in order for us to maximize our well-being. However, remember that you can't expect perfection. The point is not that we have to ceaselessly strive for unattainable goals of perfect body, perfect relationships . . . perfect anything. The point is that we are our own ecosystems. We need to pursue balance and harmony.

A health improvement in any one domain will magnify and accelerate your gains in the other two.

This need for balance is true in ways that are very exciting: If you improve each aspect of your whole person, not only will you be happier generally, but a health improvement in any one domain will magnify and accelerate your gains in the other two. There is a direct line of cause and effect. Quit smoking and your social, mental and spiritual health will all improve. Make a new friend and engage in healthy social activity and you will positively change your physical and spiritual well-being. Learn something new that expands your mind and you will reap better physical, social and spiritual health. Experience a deep spiritual realization of connectedness with the earth and watch your physical and mental health improve.

Let me illustrate the interdependency of our domains with an example. If my habits change in one small area—I walk up a flight of stairs to the lunchroom at work, breaking free of a prior habit of taking the elevator—then my whole person grows in health. By walking up 13 steps, my body gets a surge of positive physical stimulation. I experience increased oxygen intake from my exertion. This air floods my entire bloodstream—not just to the leg muscles that "needed" the oxygen to climb the stairs, but also my face and brain. As I enter the lunchroom, my complexion is slightly improved due to the oxygen-enriched blood now coursing through my veins. I feel a bit energized—an effect from released hormones. I greet a colleague and my improved complexion combined with the energy in my voice immediately makes me more attractive than I would ordinarily be. My colleague responds warmly and we begin to chat as we queue in the cafeteria line. With the blood that has come to my brain and the small release of positive hormones, I am quicker thinking and, therefore, more engaging. This small positive interaction, in turn, impacts my spiritual well-being because I was connected to another being in a harmonious way. And there you have it! The simple act of one small improvement in one domain of our person improves all domains that make up our whole person.

In the pages to follow, I will try to briefly re-emphasize this point again and again. You are your own ecosystem. Due to the principle of interdependency of domains, every step you take to improve one part of this ecosystem will improve all parts of it.

There are, however, two paradoxes we need to explore: limitations and lack of moderation.

Limitations

At the beginning of this chapter, I offered a simple introduction to Plato's Theory of Forms—the idea that one's mental picture of an object is always a more perfect version than an example from our sensory reality. This theory of forms applies to our own happier, healthier selves. What we envision for ourselves will take shape in the real outward expression of our lives, but there are practical limitations for us all.

I can envision myself as a muscular, world class body builder but I will never be one. My parents passed to me DNA (basic genetic programming) that has led to shoulders that are average in width and a limited capacity for muscle gain. There is no protein supplement, steroid or weight-lifting technique that will expand the skeletal width of my shoulders. With deliberate exercise I can improve the bone density within my shoulders and I could certainly add a lot more muscle mass. However, no matter how hard I strive towards it, I will never have the physique of a world class body builder.

My conception of my perfect self—per the Theory of Forms—must accept and know the bounds of my potential. I cannot beneficially envision myself with 50 inch width shoulders. That would be like the mathematician trying to envision a triangle with four sides. One's vision for one's self must accept the limits of reality; however—and this is really important—one's vision must not impose limits that are not there. Consider this statement: "I will never fly by flapping my arms. Gravity and my anatomy will limit me". This recognition of a limit is valid. "I will never be fit" is unlikely to be a valid limit for most readers. Do not define your potential by limits that are not real.

When we envision our perfect selves, let us be kind and compassionate towards our own limitations. Let us NOT make limits where they don't exist, but have the wisdom and humility to easily embrace and accept the limits we do have. Once we have done so, we see our whole person and the potential for wellness we each have. We will still strive for a balanced internal ecosystem consisting of health in all three domains; however, in cases of substantial limitations we must accept what we have to work with. Once we accept our limitations, we can move forward with our goals. Examples abound of individuals who overcome their substantial disabilities and far exceed the expectations others have for them.

My experience, both in my own life and in working with clients, has consistently shown the greatest limits are those we have constructed in our own minds. Would it not be more constructive and empowering to envision your perfect self and strive towards that, whilst accepting the modest limitations that do exist. To apply Plato's Theory of Forms—to envision your perfect self—is within reach for the vast majority of our society. Your potential perfect self lies ahead but first we must address the second paradox.

Lack of Moderation

A colleague I used to work with could run 10 miles at blazing speed. She also cycled and lifted weights. I knew her for more than 10 years. She would regularly run into work (40 minutes), go to the gym at lunch (50 minutes) and then run home at the end of the day (another 40 minutes). She was proud of her body and wore flattering skirts and blouses. Her dark hair was nicely styled, cut and dyed with auburn high-lights. She didn't wear a lot of make-up but her eyes were carefully prepared with mascara and eye shadow. She looked good.

I don't know much about her personal life except that she had a history of failed romantic partnerships and she struggled to guide the development of her two children. I don't believe her life was very happy—in fact, I know it wasn't. She was often bitter and took considerable time off work for mental health issues. Her personal life was clearly tumultuous.

Notably, when the man she was living with left her, her coping mechanism was more exercise. She ran farther, training for a marathon. She also took up cycling in a more intense way while continuing her routine of weight-lifting. Her life appeared to revolve around maximizing her physical fitness.

She was, and possibly still is, a junkie, constantly craving the high she got from exercise. I have no doubt the exercise made her feel good. It was happiness of a sort— a substitute for true well-being.

This woman's happiness fell short of meeting some very real needs. Her capacity to get pleasure and contentment from her physical activity was very real. Biochemically, she experienced tremendous surges of dopamine during and immediately following her exercise. Dopamine is a natural chemical neurotransmitter created in the body through exercise. It is one of the most powerful activators of the brain's pleasure centers. Dopamine is chemically similar to addictive opioids such as morphine.

In times of stress, my colleague undoubtedly felt some relief through her exercise. When her relationship with her partner ended, increasing her already intense regimen may have assisted her in coping with her relationship failure. However, I expect her life was not well balanced.

As a full-time employee and a single mother of two children, at what cost did her exercise come? I wonder if her life had any spare time for growing in all her domains. By throwing herself into exercise she provided herself relief from emotional pain, ignoring the underlying causes by applying a salve of dopamine-induced pleasure. She was treating the symptoms but was unlikely to address the disease.

I know another woman who has dropped in and out of mainstream society several times, taking years of her life to withdraw into meditation. She has a long history of failed relationships, lives apart from her young son (whom she misses terribly) and can't sustain meaningful employment.

She appears to be a spiritual master of sorts. She can quote Tibetan religious texts and describe in detail many different meditation techniques. She also knows the essential teachings of many modern spiritual leaders. And yet, she remains unhappy and generally depressed. Her spiritualism has not given her the benefit that true spiritual masters achieve. Rather than using spiritual reflection to better manage her whole life, she has substituted deep spiritualism for a whole and balanced life. She hides from confronting and improving the other domains of her life. No matter how spiritually strong she tries to be, she can't be healthy or happy without successful engagement in her other domains.

These two extreme examples—the tireless fitness colleague and the depressed spiritual seeker—demonstrate the importance of maintaining a reasonable balance in our pursuits. With an overemphasis on growth and mastery in one domain, invariably the other domains suffer and thus the whole person suffers.

The road to well-being is different for each of us. As individuals, we will find and pursue our own methods to improve each of our domains, and we must pursue balance in EACH domain. Inattention to any one domain will result in disharmony and a lack of overall well-being. Anyone interested in improving their life must commit to developing in all three domains.

Of course, each person brings their own personality and character strengths to their life's journey. Some may be naturally more inclined to a strong social life, others to physical activity, and still others to spiritual or intellectual pursuits. There may be differences amongst us in emphasis on one domain or another, which is completely normal and expected. So long as an emphasis on one domain or another is moderate, then a balanced well-being can be achieved.

Mastery

I have used the word "mastery" many times over and will continue to do so throughout the pages of this book. It is therefore worthwhile to pause and ensure a shared understanding of the use of this word.

A dictionary defines mastery as an expert level of knowledge or skill in a subject area. When one has mastered a subject, one has a significant level of accomplishment.

Mastery, as a concept, is a relative idea. We can master component parts of a topic yet have far to go with respect to all aspects of the topic. For example, a toddler will master the process of differentiating between "more" and "all gone". A parent will ask again and again, "Do you want more?" And the child will reach out to receive another spoonful of food. When this youngster reaches out and the parent says "all gone", the child learns there is no more of the particular food. This is genuinely a mastery of an essential mathematical equation—more is greater than zero (all gone).

In this way we are all constantly in mid-process towards greater mastery. A toddler will grow in his or her mathematical prowess. By the age of three many children will have learned to count to ten and will understand that each ascending numeral is one greater than the previous ordered number. Similarly, a 50-year-old professor may solve a mathematical theorem of great complexity and be said to have "mastered" it. So mastery is a process all people are engaged in throughout their lives.

Mastery, of course, also has a substantial range of subjects, each of which in turn have an endless division of component parts. Math, as a subject, has many sub-topics—calculus, geometry, algebra, etc.—just as cooking has innumerable techniques—frying, marinading, curing, pickling, etc.

With regard to the three domains of our lives—body, mind and spirit—each represents its own broad subject and each subject, in turn, has myriad component parts. Our physical domain consists of sub-topics such as nutrition, exercise and sleep. Each sub-topic can be broken down further. Exercise, for example, can be split into cardio-vascular, strength training, endurance and so on.

Right now each of us has some level of accomplishment in each of our three domains. One purpose of this book is to make you conscious of where you stand in terms of your own mastery of each domain. Some readers will be accomplished athletes while others have profound spiritual lives. Still others may have highly stimulated mental conditions. As you move through the chapters of this book, you are invited to take stock of your own level of mastery in each sub-topic of each do-main. Once you have identified areas where you can achieve "more", then you have found a potential source of great fulfillment. The joy in life is, in part, a function of the process of mastering.

Fun is found in the work of accomplishing things. This simple truth, if acted upon, is a major motivator for us to live fuller, more happy lives. Let me repeat this key point: Fun is found in the work (or play) of accomplishing things.

This is an extraordinarily powerful reality. Mid-life crisis—whenever it happens in life—is almost always a function of the non-realization of greater mastery and/or the complete lack of appreciation for the topics where we are achieving greater mastery. The 45-year-old office worker who has stayed in the same job for many years may be in the middle part of his parenting years with little time for personal interests. The funk that many people experience at this stage in their lives is simply understood to be a function of a deprivation from the normal process of mastering. Contrast this with children who cannot help but be engaged in this process across many facets of their lives. Post mid-life most adults must either take on new challenges or "settle" for what is. This book will provide all readers—no matter their age—options for pursuing mastery.

The leading researcher on this topic of mastery is psychologist, Dr. Mihaly Csikszentmihaly. His 2008 book, *Flow: The Psychology of Optimal Experience*, was the product, of 35 years of research into the happy state of "doing". He states: "It is by being fully involved in every detail of our lives, whether good or bad, that we find happiness, not by trying to look for it directly."

Being fully involved in the detail of our lives is simply the on-going process of learning—growing in one or more areas of our lives. It is in our discipline and dedication to this process of growing that we achieve happiness.

Csikszentmihaly notes that when we are in the act of mastering something— anything that is voluntary, worthwhile and has a component of challenge to it—we experience the blissful state known as "flow". We have all experienced this. I would like you to bring a memory of this to your mind. Remember a time when you were fully engrossed in your activity: any activity at all. It could be a time you were playing a sport, cooking, praying, solving a crossword puzzle—anything. When you are in flow, nothing distracts your attention. You have excellent concentration. You persist even though there is some challenge in what you are doing. You sense that, on the one hand you are learning and, on the other hand, you are doing your task with a sense of accomplishment and achievement. You are in the act of mastering something.

An example of flow in my own life is when I play sports against someone who generally matches my skill level. If I am playing competitively with an opponent in tennis who is much less skilled than me, the activity is less fun because there isn't enough of a challenge to grow my skills. If I am playing with someone much more skilled than I am, the tennis game lacks enjoyment because I am too easily beaten and, again, I am learning very little. The ideal state of flow is when I am challenged to the point that my skills are continually being called upon to sharpen in order to stay closely matched with my competitor.

I also experience flow when I am coaching a client who is particularly stuck in a life challenge. My curiosity is piqued. I know that my inquiries must be sharp and effective. I am eager, leaning forward and listening intently. I celebrate when my client makes a breakthrough and discovers something powerful about who they are or where they need to go.

When you are in a state of flow, time becomes less important. You may completely lose track of it because your task has so fully absorbed your attention. Typically, you know what you are trying to accomplish in fairly certain terms. Your

goal is clear. You lose yourself in the experience. You do not consider your mood while you are in the midst of the activity. It is upon its conclusion that you recognize the inner sense of accomplishment and joy that was derived from your efforts.

States of flow can be found in something that is time bound and purposeful—such as a tennis game—or in activity that can be spontaneous and fluid—such as striking up an interesting conversation with a stranger you have just met. Flow can also be achieved in slow and deliberate processes like meditation, painting and even reading a book. Flow can be found in almost any activity when the right ingredients are there, including a sincere desire to be doing the activity, a level of challenge that stimulates growth, and a clear sense of purpose with built-in feedback to let you know if you are accomplishing your goals or not. Finally, an activity with flow requires heightened concentration. A happy activity rarely happens when one's attention is constantly interrupted.

A meaningful, happy life comes through engaging flow activities. Body, mind and spirit are broad labels over many related components of our lives. Our physical domain is a label to describe activities such as sleeping, eating and exercising. The mind domain is a label to describe activities including being with friends, embracing culture and enjoying family. It's activities in our lives that make us happy. If we know we need to aim toward flow activities in each domain, our pursuit of happiness is much easier.

Set your target on flow activities. By consciously considering the essential ingredients of flow, you can plan your engagement in the activities described in the upcoming chapters with purpose and confidence. Essential flow ingredients are:

1. **Volunteering** — Even when you "have to" do something (like go to work or wash the dishes) you get to choose your approach and attitude. The more you make yourself a volunteer for what is happening in your life, the happier you will be. This does not mean you should settle and be complacent about what is undesirable. Instead, work to remove major obstacles to happiness without rejecting what is actually happening in any given moment. For example, if your job is wasting your talents and your colleagues are miserable to be with, make a plan to get a different job (more on this later). But until you get that new job, volunteer yourself to be at your current job in a way that is as engaging as you can make it. See if you can improve some aspect of your productivity. Challenge yourself to make one colleague cheerier. Choose what you can do to make that activity better and enjoy whatever good is present.

2. **Being purposeful and goal-oriented** — Set goals that have reasonable ways of measuring achievement. Big goals are good, but you must be able to break any big project down into small enough milestones so you can see progression or a lack thereof. If you don't know how you are doing in an activity, you won't find it rewarding for long.

3. **Engaging in challenge** — Stretch your current skills (or level of achievement) without overwhelming yourself. Almost any worthwhile undertaking can have the right amount of challenge as long as you think through the path to betterment clearly enough. The activity must be suited to your current level of development. The challenge must propel you forward rather than serve as a source of discouragement.

4. **Concentrating** — Flow does not often happen in environments where there is constant multi-tasking and disruption. It can happen in busy, noisy environments, but you must be able to maintain concentration on what is important. Imagine an air traffic control job in which information that requires split second decisions is constantly coming in. This noisy, busy environment may very well provide opportunity for flow. However, an air traffic controller who has the simultaneous chore of child minding toddlers will not have flow (in which case, I don't want to be in an approaching aircraft). We need a reasonable learning environment to grow during flow activities.

Armed with the knowledge of flow and the joy that comes with purposeful activity, we are ready to start on the substantive journey into the three domains of our lives.

PART ONE

Body: Physical Well-being

This section of the book examines our physical selves and is the subject of six short chapters. Each chapter describes how to attain foundational health in these necessary areas:

- Fitness

- Nutrition

- Sleep/rest and sex

- Preventing disease and aging well

- Money/meeting our material needs

- Safety and security

Few of us will master these six areas of health. However, we must achieve some level of success in each category because any singular deficit will bring down our whole self like a house of cards. To illustrate, our pursuit of personal happiness is pointless and impossible to achieve if we are chronically under slept and stressed out. Part One of this book offers a "happy" path to health and all basic areas of our physical well-being.

3 Fitness

We all know that getting off the couch and doing something for our bodies is good for us. Why do so many of us struggle with this simple action?

The truth is that, for many of us, it's not simple. We have busy lives that afford little time to exercise. And we are exhausted by the time we get home from work, eat dinner and attend to the myriad tasks that our lives demand from us. Getting exercise is desirable, but it's not always easy to find the time or the willpower to get to it. It's just one more demand that—at least for now—has to get in line behind a host of other obligations we must attend to.

I'm sympathetic to this point of view. I've been there during more than one period in my life. I distinctly remember a specific moment of surprise and deep learning when I was 35 years old. I had always seen myself as an athlete. This was a fundamental component of my identity. I grew up with a sport for every season. I rode my bike everywhere as a kid and all through my university years. I thought of myself as fit.

At 35, I was also a dad of two young sons, a dedicated manager of a busy office, and a home-owner with many do-it-yourself projects on the go. After the kids were put to bed with love, attention and numerous bedtime stories, I would—at last—have some down time. My former wife and I would often enjoy a movie or we would quietly read together before we went off to bed.

One evening after the kids were in bed, I was lying down on the couch with a book propped on my belly. Wait... what? A belly? I had never seen it before. For all my life, I had only known this perfectly flat surface decorated with a few hairs and a belly button. But suddenly, as I gazed down at my prone figure, I realized there was something different. My belly was soft and round and made an upward bulge where my flat bookshelf ought to have been. I have to admit I was amused at first. I, the athlete, had a soft, round belly.

I contemplated for a moment how an athlete like me could develop this belly fat. I don't suppose I had weighed myself in years and certainly didn't see a progression to having a belly. But suddenly I had one. I considered my circumstances and slowly realized I was not an athlete…not even close. I played no sports and hadn't for years. I didn't run, walk or jog anywhere. My old, beloved bike was in a shed behind numerous other objects that had prime locations because I actually used them, quite unlike my bike.

Now, I was relatively lucky. I was perhaps only 10 pounds overweight and I loved to play sports. I gave some thought to what I would like to do to get myself in shape. As a boy, I played countless hours of road hockey. My mom had avoided signing me up for real ice hockey. I think she was terrified I would get injured. She was also a single parent to six kids, of which I was the youngest. She was exceptionally generous to us all, but she had limited capacity to shepherd me around to hockey rinks for practices and games.

I looked at my community recreation guide and found a "Learn to Play Hockey" program. Voila! Within a year, I was in excellent shape, playing hockey a few nights per week with a couple different teams. What's more is that I was having a great time doing it. Hockey was fun. The adrenalin rush that comes with high speeds, rapturous victories and desolate defeats was a blast.

I played hockey for nine years in a row, eight months of each year. It became a regular part of my weekly routine. My teammates knew they could count on me to show up consistently. I even scheduled business trips—as best I could—to accommodate my hockey schedule. When I tore the ligaments in my knee during a particularly scrappy game, my three month rehab was motivated by an unspoken, yet clear commitment to return to the ice.

Hockey became a meaningful part of my lifestyle. I designed my life activities to include hockey as part of an integrated day-to-day approach.

Lifestyle is defined as the way a person lives. Lifestyle characterizes who we are and what's important to us. If our actions define who we really are, then our lifestyle is the outward expression of our innermost being. Hockey became a part of how I defined my own identity.

Fitness can't be sustained in any meaningful way if it isn't incorporated as part of our lifestyle. Let me repeat this for emphasis: Personal fitness has to be who you are as expressed in outward behaviors in order for it to be sustainable.

Lifestyle characterizes who we are and what's important to us.

If you have a level of reasonable fitness now, you already have lifestyle components that promote fitness. Expand and invest in the activities you do or would like to do in order to pursue your fitness goals. Put your energies into activities that already seem congruent with your lifestyle.

If your current level of fitness is poor and has never been great, you will need to give more energy and attention to the pursuit of your goals. Adding a new and foreign activity into your lifestyle is harder than leaning into existing behavior patterns. You will have a more concrete and substantive lifestyle change. While this is harder to do, the satisfaction as you progress toward fitness will be hugely rewarding!

Accomplishing fitness goals may also be easier than you think. The world over, for all of history, the vast majority of humans have been naturally fit. Farmers in ancient Egypt didn't go to the gym. Shepherds in England didn't hire personal trainers. Native fishermen on the coasts of North America didn't buy exercise bikes for their homes. How did all these people maintain fitness? They just went about their daily lives with the normal activities required of them. Farmers broke land, planted seeds and harvested grain. Shepherds walked and rested. Fishermen paddled boats, and cast out and hauled in nets. Fitness flowed from their lifestyles. These ancient and not so ancient peoples also danced, played games, made love, and pursued crafts and other hobbies.

For you? The same. Do what people have done across the ages. Engage in living.

If going to the gym is your idea of play, then by all means do that. If running a few miles every morning is your meditation and liberation, then run. If shooting hockey pucks or dribbling in for a 2-point lay-up is your thing, haul out your skates or running shoes and head to the nearest recreation center.

If none of these common sporty activities has any appeal for you, there are countless other ways to find fitness. The key is finding activities that make you happy. The things that make you happy are things you will do over and over again. And things done repeatedly are your lifestyle.

Need some ideas?

Walk in nature — People everywhere are drawn to natural environments. A walk in a forest smells good. Plants are endlessly varied and can be subtly evocative. Occasionally, squirrels and birds enliven the scenery. Leaves whisper in a light breeze. Water trickles over rocks and fallen branches. Sunshine filters onto our faces and warms our skin. If you live near a park or other natural setting, you could readily incorporate this experience into your regular day-to-day life. Likely, there are many people near you who also love to walk in nature. Grab a friend or family member and enjoy the natural world.

Plant a garden — Raspberries come in huge numbers every July at my house. I love them. My kids reluctantly do as they are told when I send them outside to pick berries. They come back smiling, with bowls full of berries and tummies filled with sweetness. Putting handfuls of well-aged compost around my bedding plants is a rite of spring for me. The smell of the pure earth is as good as anything. Turning the soil with a spade is tremendously exhilarating. I cheer for each worm brought to the surface. May you be well, worm! Farming is what I am doing physically, but playing is more like it. Flowers and veggies, water and dirt, shovels and rakes, new plants and old—a garden is richly stimulating.

Commute on foot or by bike: Are you tied to your car? Do you suffer in bumper to bumper traffic? It's amazing how much more there is in the world when you remove yourself from the cocoon of a car and instead explore your neighborhood in a much richer way. Be in the fresh air, see the people, notice the seasons progressing bit by bit, day by day. I like to escort my younger son to school by bike. I am surprised at how wonderful it is. I greet the same people over and over again with a cheerful "Good Morning"! I actually think that, incrementally, we are changing the culture of the urban route on which we commute. People are learning to be friendly. And when I walk along the same trail I bike on, the slower pace reveals things I didn't notice before. Changing the way you commute to work is perhaps one of the most progressive ways for you to change your lifestyle. It's relatively easy to make it a habit because the habit of going to work is already well established. Cycling or walking is environmentally friendly, social and invigorating. And when you arrive at work, you will be mentally sharper. If you live too far away to walk or bike, then park your car part way between home and work. If you take the bus, get off several stops early and walk the rest of the way.

Other possibilities: Walk a dog–your own or a neighbor's. Take a dance class.

Start a paper route. Go to art galleries and museums. Wander in heritage home neighborhoods. Any and all of these activities, when done regularly as part of your lifestyle, are enough to make you fit.

Get Real!

Let's pause here for a moment and think about what we mean by fitness. If you are like most people, the concept of fitness has a comic book image with it—Superman, Batman, Wonder-woman, The Hulk or Captain America. These characters are ultra lean, with ripped abs and superhuman powers. They are fit, but they are also imaginary.

Fitness in our imaginations should ideally match what is attainable in our real lives. At the beginning of this book I noted that I would never be a world class bodybuilder; not even if I trained all day, every day. I simply am not built with wide enough shoulders. And frankly, I have no desire to look like Schwarzenegger or a superhero. Fit for me means I have adequate lung and heart capacity such that I could run after a dog that bolts away. It means I am strong enough to turn over a good chunk of the vegetable garden in a single session. It means being flexible enough that I can sit cross-legged on the floor. I want to look reasonably healthy. I want to feel energetic.

What does fit mean for you? Really think about this. If you have an impossible image of who you "should" be, take the time now to extend yourself some kindness. I want to especially say this to women, who are subject to relentless images of a singular standard of beauty. TV, magazines, mannequins and almost all public images of idealized women shows femininity as an unrealistic body type. The idealized image of women is unhealthy and drives many people to tragic eating disorders in a relentless pursuit of thinness. Imagery of frail, gaunt women abound in popular culture. Men are, to a lesser extent, subject to this same societal pressure to fit a singular macho body type.

Let it go! See yourself for who you are. Look closely. Are you overweight, weak and easily winded by exercise? What standard are you setting? What would it be like to be less overweight, yet imperfect. What would it be like to be stronger, yet still carry body fat? What would it be like to have more heart and lung capacity, yet still not be a marathon runner? Tune up an image of your future self that is kind and realistic and decidedly not an image that is put upon you by external influences. It does not take hours in a gym, or miles of running to be fit. Consider again people from historical times who simply went about the activities of their lives, which required manual labor. They were fit. Include some manual activity in your life, things you enjoy and that make sense to incorporate into your lifestyle.

A few tips

If this topic of fitness is particularly daunting for you, take heart. It may be less challenging than you think.

Make choices consistent with your lifestyle — Lots of research has been done on the subject of exercise and motivating consistent behavior. This is why I emphasize incorporating exercise as a harmonious part of your lifestyle. Exercise is rarely maintained over the long run if the activity chosen is something we don't like and is burdensome to fit into our lives.

Pre-decision — There is an approach to behavior change I call pre-decision. It is when you make decisions well in advance of the moment when you need to act on the decision. For example, I may decide today what I will do tomorrow at noon. We are all familiar with this ordinary way of approaching the normal activities of our lives. This is as simple as keeping a calendar. Tomorrow at 10, I have an appointment with the dental hygienist. By putting the appointment in my calendar, I have effectively decided what my behavior will be tomorrow at 10. Our commitment to a fit lifestyle requires the same kind of advance decision-making.

If my exercise regimen is dependent on how I feel or what I want to do sometime vaguely later today, then I am much less likely to act the way I would like to. On the other hand, if I decide first thing in the morning that I will change my regular commute to work by getting off the bus two stops early and walking the remaining way, then my behavior is more automated and consistent when I actually arrive at the appropriate bus stop. Similarly, if I commit to meet my friend for a walk this evening at 7, I am much more likely to actually do it than if I wait until 7 tonight and ponder whether I should phone my friend and ask if they want to go for a walk.

When you pre-decide your future behaviors, you reduce the likelihood you'll renege on your commitment. The clearer and more explicit your decision, the better it will be in terms of follow through. Saying "I will exercise after work tonight" doesn't have as much certainty or energy as "I will arrive at home at 5:10 and walk to the park and back before dinner".

Enlist a friend — People who get their exercise from team sports are often unconscious of what an effective motivator their loyalty to their friends is. During my hockey playing years, I rarely missed a game even though our ice times were often late at night—sometimes after 11 o'clock—or very early in the morning—as early as 6 o'clock. I so very often didn't feel like going to the rink at the time I needed to leave, but I was committed to my team; they were counting on me to show up. So I went. And almost without fail, I was glad I did.

If team sports are not your thing, there are likely countless other people near you who also want to get a bit more fit. If you can plan a walking group with colleagues at lunch or with neighbors in the evening, you will be amazed at how much fun the engagement can be. Moreover, you will rarely, if ever, renege on your commitment.

Assuming that you love animals, and noting all the obligations of pet ownership, having a dog to walk twice daily is a great way to get yourself moving. And if you do want to be a gym rat, but are having trouble making it a habit, consider hiring a personal trainer. He or she will be at the gym at the appointed time earning your money. I expect you will be there too.

In up-coming chapters of this book, I will provide more tips on how to remain motivated and instill new behaviors. These later tips will often apply equally to your fitness goals as they do to other personal behavior changes.

Points to ponder:

- What physical activities did you enjoy as a kid? How could you get some aspects of those activities now?

- How could you change up your commute to work so that it includes exercise?

- If you are not a regular exerciser, what activity can you commit to do in the next 24 hours? Write it down, schedule and do it!

4 Nutrition

Volumes of books have been written about healthy diets. Countless articles appear in newspapers every day, excitedly reporting some new trend of scientific finding related to food. Who can argue with the importance of the subject? But it's not really so hard to wrap our heads around the facts of good eating. This chapter may seem to some readers like a basic primer, yet I genuinely believe most of us need to know nothing more about food than what is contained in the next several pages.

Know the basics about healthy food

There are countless studies and competing views on what constitutes a healthy diet. Tragically, the word diet has come to generally refer to somewhat bizarre weight loss methodologies. Most of the "diet industry" is terribly unhealthy and deliberately self-serving with a claim to have a unique and better solution for people wanting to lose weight. When I use the word "diet" here, I mean it as a reference to the usual array of foods we consume. A healthy diet, combined with physical activity, is all a body needs.

A healthy diet is less confusing than the competing food gurus would have us believe. This idea is supported by a good deal of consensus science; that is, the science that experts generally agree is well-founded by research and long-term studies. Not surprisingly, we all know most of the basics: fruits and vegetables are nutritious, whole grains are better than processed grains, low glycemic foods are better than high glycemic ones, and there is a difference between healthy fats and not-so-healthy fats. Let's examine each of these in a bit more detail.

Fruits and Vegetables are our nutritional best friends

Fruits and vegetables are food rock stars! These foods, compared to any other category of food, are extraordinarily rich in vitamins and minerals. Our bodies have complicated biological processes that are dependent on specific nutrients, including vitamins and minerals. Without these essential elements, we get weak, sick and, ultimately, we die. For example, without Vitamin C, we get scurvy, which is a deadly disease that used to kill sailors who had no access to fresh fruit and vegetables. Several B vitamins help the body release nutrients from the food we consume. Iron is required for our blood to carry oxygen. Without adequate vitamins and minerals, our bodies simply don't work. The best way to get these essential elements is through our diet. Most, but not all, essential vitamins and minerals can be found in fruit and vegetables.

We only need relatively small amounts of vitamins and minerals. Most people with a healthy and varied diet get all the vitamins and minerals they need. Supplements are unnecessary unless you have a medical condition that causes your body to be deficient in something. Moreover, supplements don't account for the interdependence between nutrients. When we take synthetic vitamins, we don't get the other chemicals that occur naturally in whole foods. For example, phytochemicals that occur naturally in many foods, don't come in a typical vitamin supplement. We know that, in some cases, the body will not absorb the vitamin without the presence of the phytochemical. Along with phytochemicals, natural fruit and vegetables have carotenoids and fibre. It is the interplay between these essential nutrients that leads to good health. Supplements cannot replicate this. Only if you have a particular deficiency, should you really need supplements. (Full disclosure: I take a multi-vitamin once a day. It is like an insurance policy, but unnecessary).

In general, the brighter colored fruits and vegetables are more nutrient-rich than others; however, the key is really to eat a diverse variety. As a bonus, they are flavorful, fresh and delicious.

Whole Grains are Best

Whole grains are superior to refined grains. A whole grain is exactly what it sounds like. The entire grain is present, including the bran, germ and endosperm. Refined grains have the germ and bran removed. Refined grains include white flour, white breads and white rice. Whole grains can be found in everything these days.

Pasta, cereal and all kinds of breads can be made with whole grains. Even white bread can be found that is made of whole wheat. Of course, whole grains are obviously found in their pure form, such as whole grain flour, brown rice, buckwheat, oatmeal, barley, quinoa and wild rice.

Whole grains retain much more nutrient value compared to refined grains. That means you get more vitamins, minerals and antioxidants when these foods are consumed. In addition, they have more fibre and protein. The fibre from whole grains has many benefits, including keeping your bowel movements regular, reducing cardio-vascular risks and aiding in the digestion of other foods.

Low Glycemic carbohydrates provide stable energy

Low glycemic foods are better than high glycemic foods. Carbohydrates such as breads, pasta, cereals and other starchy foods are basic sources for energy. These foods are dense and provide many calories. Carbohydrates are generally a major fuel for our body's many needs. For this reason, athletes talk about 'carb-ing up' before a workout. They eat high energy foods so their bodies have the energy to do the work that they set out to do. But not all carbs deliver energy the same way.

High glycemic foods are converted quickly into blood sugar. They boost our energy in a hurry. On some occasions this is fine. For example, during an extended workout you may need instant energy and a high-glycemic snack will be just the right thing. However, if you are not preparing for a workout you will likely feel worse after eating high-glycemic foods. For example, 20 minutes after you eat a sugary donut made of refined white flour, you get a huge rush of energy. This high-glycemic snack is processed quickly and almost instantly is converted into lots of available energy for our bodies. But wait another 20 minutes and the blood sugar crashes and you feel lethargic. What happened?

High glycemic foods such as refined grains found in many breads and cereals, sugars (including natural ones in fruit), potatoes and corn chips, release their energy quickly into the blood stream. When that energy doesn't get used, the body's response is to crank up its production of insulin, which converts the high sugar content in our blood to storage as fat. This spike in insulin then crashes the blood sugar, leading to a tired, foggy feeling. Unhealthy diets with lots of high glycemic foods, leads to a rollercoaster ride of daily highs and lows. When we are in the lows, we often reach for more snacks to pick us back up. For this reason, high calorie, high glycemic foods lead to unwanted weight gain.

What we really want is energy delivered steadily over a protracted period. Low glycemic foods do just that. They move through our digestive tracts more slowly and release sugar into the bloodstream over longer periods. This leads to a more stable level of blood sugar, causing fewer energy highs and lows. Moreover, our bodies and minds feel fresh and able to work and concentrate for lengthy periods of time. When we eat lots of low glycemic foods, we are less likely to feel like snacking and we can more readily move through the day cheerfully on just three good meals. Low glycemic foods include nuts, legumes, most pasta, whole grains like brown rice and oatmeal, most vegetables and dairy products.

Not all Fats are created equal

We need fats as part of a healthy diet. They keep our skin soft and pliable, they deliver certain fat-soluble vitamins, and they are an excellent source of energy. However, not all fats are created equal. Essentially, there are two kinds of fats: saturated and unsaturated. Within each of these categories, there are sub-categories, but it doesn't need to get too complex.

Saturated fats are associated with cardio-vascular disease, diabetes and several types of cancer. They come from animal products and a few vegetable sources, such as coconut oil and palm oil. These fats are strongly associated with high cholesterol, which can lead to cardiovascular disease.

Good fats are unsaturated fats that come primarily from vegetables and some fish oils. When we consume unsaturated fats, we lower our risk for cardiovascular disease. Try olive or canola oils when your recipe calls for fats. And eat fish once or twice a week.

Eat three proper meals per day

Everyone has heard the maxim that breakfast is the most important meal of the day. It's true. All night long our bodies use the energy attained from your evening food. By morning, we are depleted of energy. A healthy, hearty breakfast kick starts our entire physical being. It fires up our digestive system. The first process that is undertaken is replenishing the body's hydration. Through the night, we respire a lot of liquid from our bodies and upon awakening we empty our bladders. We are typically most dehydrated in the early morning. This is why most heart attacks happen in the early morning—our blood is thick and sluggish. By rehydrating straight away, we loosen joints and energize organs, including our brains, which work better when we are well hydrated.

As our digestive system fires up, so does our cardiovascular system. Digesting food is hard work and requires the energy provided by oxygen-rich blood—lots of it! With a good breakfast in your tummy, your heart beats a little faster and your rate of respiration goes up. In short, you really wake up.

Eating breakfast is highly correlated with reduced impulse consumption. This is critical for well-being. Nothing contributes to unhealthy eating as much as the food we consume without planning and proper consideration. Without breakfast in our bellies, all of us are easily tempted by the morning donut, sugar-filled muffin or chocolate bar. How could we not be? This desire to eat what is convenient and packed with calories is not just tempting, it is our body's most basic survival need. We must eat! Deprived of a healthy start to the day, we will take whatever is readily available when hunger overpowers rational food consumption; that is, the reptilian brain, when pressed on matters of basic survival, will win nearly every argument with the more developed but subservient primate brain. When we start the day without breakfast, we don't just succumb to impulse eating in mid-morning. We tend to fall into unthoughtful eating through the whole day—a snack mid-morning, a late lunch that may resemble a big snack, and more big food cravings in the afternoon, which again may be satisfied by impulse eating.

Eating breakfast is highly correlated with reduced impulse consumption.

Eat three meals a day, including a proper breakfast. So what is a proper breakfast? A proper breakfast needs to fill the empty belly with about 500 calories—more for big men and very active athletes. Fortunately, there are hundreds if not thousands of healthy choices for us. If you don't have your own plans already, consider these options:

- A medium-sized apple (80 calories), two pieces of whole wheat toast topped with unsweetened peanut butter (340 calories), and a glass of soy milk (110 calories) or 1% cow's milk (110 calories). Total = 530 calories

- A large orange (90 calories), followed by one and a half cups of oatmeal (250 calories) with a ½ cup of frozen blueberries cooked in (40 calories) and topped with almond milk (60 calories) and one and a half tablespoons of pumpkin seeds (90 calories). Total = 530 calories

- In a big hurry? Break two bananas (220 calories) into chunks and toss into a blender, pour in a cup of soy milk (110 calories), add a ¾ cup of 0% fat Greek yogurt (70 calories) and three ice cubes. I love to add spinach or kale to my smoothies. Blend. Total = 400 calories

- Three whole grain homemade pancakes (270 calories) with a modest three tablespoons of maple syrup (150 calories) and with a generous ¾ cup serving of fresh berries (80 calories). Total = 500 calories.

Note that spreading on a tablespoon of margarine (70 calories) or butter (100 calories) adds a lot more caloric content.

- A banana (110 calories) along with a bowl of healthy breakfast cereal, such as Kashi Go Lean (200 calories) and a cup of 1% cow's milk (110 calories) or soy milk (110 calories). Total = 420 calories

Healthy, easy breakfasts like these help you start the day with the energy you need. Importantly, this start will also keep you away from sugary snacks.

Eat lunch and dinner as close to the same times of day as you can manage. Try to plan your meals. I am sometimes poor at thinking ahead, but I have a number of default options for all my meals. When I'm pressed for time or lacking inspiration, I pick a healthy default lunch or dinner option. The important thing is that I maintain control over what goes into my body. I do not resort to ordering pizza or driving through a fast food joint due to a lack of planning or inability to put together a good meal.

If you stick to eating three good meals per day—at regular times every day—your body will have substantially fewer cravings and binge temptations.

Keep healthy foods on hand

I was in a well-known discount retailer with a buggy full of groceries one day, and as I proceeded through the checkout, the cashier commented that in his entire tenure at the store—where he had rung through tens of thousands of customers' groceries—he had never seen a healthier selection than mine. I was surprised! I hadn't been highly selective in my shopping; it was more or less the usual routine. Nevertheless, I left the store rather pleased and curious about his observation.

When I got home, as my youngest son helped me put the groceries away, I told him what the cashier had said. Then he and I discussed our purchases—about $150 worth. There were two large grocery bags filled with fruits and vegetables. One similarly large bag of four loaves of whole-grain bread made partially with quinoa flour, and a bag of whole-grain bagels. Slid alongside was a pack of whole wheat tortilla shells. In the remaining bag, there were two jugs of low-fat milk, a package of old cheddar cheese, and a large container of no-fat plain greek yogurt. In this last bag, I also had four packages of instant noodles (the kind that you just add boiling water and slice open the small flavoring packet). These unhealthy instant noodles were my only purchase from the racetrack–the inside aisles–of the store. And that is part of the secret to shopping.

Nearly all grocery stores are designed the same way—the front is dedicated to checkouts, one side is loaded with bakery products, the back has meats and dairy products, and the remaining side has fruits and vegetables. I am sure you can see the layout in your mind's eye. This layout is like a racetrack. Inside the circle is where you want to spend relatively little time. Aisle after aisle is full of highly processed concoctions filled with all manner of stuff that should not be in our diets. High levels of sugar, fat and salt are found in almost all processed foods. Why is this? They are cheap and add lots of flavor to food that is otherwise bland, overcooked and made with low-quality ingredients. In addition, processed foods are laden with ingredients that are not food: unpronounceable chemicals, additives and colorings that help fool our eyes, nose and taste buds into believing we are eating real food.

Like so many other things in this book, I am not making a wholesale recommendation that you stay out of the middle aisles. Rather, I am saying proceed with caution! There are a number of healthy middle aisle items. Frozen veggies have similar nutritional value compared to fresh and they are convenient to have on hand. Pastas, rice, quinoa, whole-grain flours, spices are also components of a healthy diet. I like to stock up on these middle-aisle items.

If you buy healthy foods and you make a point of eating at home, by default you will have a healthy diet. However, you'll need to plan your defense against the inevitable two crises:

1. No time to cook at home.

2. The overwhelming desire for a snack to go along with your evening movie (or other relaxing activity).

We need fast food. It is unavoidable and a simple reality of the busy, over-pressurized lives that so many of us endure. Two answers exist for the fast food conundrum: the first solution is like religion—obey with certainty and you will be saved. That is, if you must eat a fast-food meal, go to Subway and order a whole wheat "Veggie Delight" with a low-fat dressing. This is a healthy, quick and inexpensive meal. Of course, there are other alternatives, and no, I'm not getting a commission from Subway. Go ahead and choose an alternative, but if you go that route, keep the all-vegetable, whole wheat sandwich in mind. If your alternative genuinely compares to the blessed "Veggie Delight", have at it!

The second solution to the real need for fast food requires more planning, but is a good option. Freeze leftovers and purposely create other frozen dinners. If you are making a bean vegetable stew, double the recipe and freeze the leftovers in convenient freezer-safe containers. Make two butternut squash lasagnas rather than one. Give up a bit more time to a once-a-week meal prep event and load up on something that is healthy and that you like. Having good, prepared food on hand can be a life-saver when the alternative is a burger and fries.

What about snack time? How can I watch a movie without popcorn smothered in butter? How can friends and I play cards without potato chips? If you are generally well, not grossly overweight, or suffering from high blood pressure, diabetes, or some other chronic condition, go ahead and eat chips or popcorn. Being healthy should not mean giving up little indulgences. Conscious moderation is key.

The beauty and pleasure of a healthy lifestyle is that it does not impose harsh restrictions. But—and this is a big but—you must have a truly healthy style in your everyday, ordinary life. If you do, there are few, if any, absolute rules. It is simply that most days, most of the food we consume—most of the calories, that is—come from healthy sources. This is one of the reasons I am a fan of Dean Ornish's work. He is the doctor who has proven that chronic health conditions like diabetes and heart disease cannot only be managed, but in most cases can be reversed through diet. Dr. Ornish's recommendations are simple and easy to follow. His prescription for healthy food is broad and permissive, except in cases where the patients are in the process of overcoming serious disease. In those circumstances, it is perfectly logical that a few beers and a bag of Cheetos is off the menu. However, for people who are successful in establishing a long-term, healthy eating lifestyle, Dr. Ornish puts no constraints on eating "bad" foods. He simply notes the practical need for moderation.

Body: Physical Well-Being

You may want to pick up one of his books. *The Spectrum* is perhaps the most accessible publication about his research findings and the food lifestyle he promotes. The subtitle of the book perhaps says it all: *A Scientifically Proven Program to Feel Better, Live Longer, Lose Weight, and Gain Health.* The following overview will not do justice to the book, but it might be helpful to stimulate your thinking:

- Eat lots of good, flavorful foods. Healthy eating is not about depriving yourself of "bad" treats; after all, the occasional bit of junk food is ok. However, there are lots of foods that are flavorful and are high in nutrients. Nothing fits this bill better than fruit, vegetables and whole grains.

- Eat a variety of low-glycemic food, distributing your energy uptake over the periods between meals.

- Eat unprocessed, whole foods and eat a varied selection of foods so you consume complimentary and relatively complete nutrients. High fiber found in whole foods will keep you regular and also significantly reduce the likelihood of contracting several forms of cancer.

- Eat fun treats on occasion, being mindful of keeping these foods to moderate amounts. Savor them.

Dr. Ornish has categorized different types of food into five groups (listed below). He says a person should eat the most food from group one and the second most from group two. Partaking of food from group three should be moderate. And food eaten from groups four and five should be eaten on rare occasions. Food from groups four and five should be avoided if serious disease exists. Fortunately, there is no great mystery or complexity to the five food groups. They are easy to understand and apply in your daily life.

Group One — Mostly fruit and vegetables, whole grains, legumes (soy, lentils, peas, beans, etc.) and non-fat dairy products.

Group Two — Mainly higher fat plants like avocados, seeds and nuts. In addition, small amounts of high-calorie fats, such as canola oil, fall into this group.

Group Three — Some cold water fish and seafood, reduced fat dairy products such as 2% milk and low-fat yogurt, margarine, and small amounts of sweeteners such as corn syrup.

Group Four — Poultry, whole milk dairy, mayonnaise and fatty seafood such as oysters.

Group Five — The least healthful foods. These include red meat, fried poultry, butter, cream, tropical oils such as palm oil, and sweets such as pastries, cakes and cookies.

You can download a graphic of this food guide from the resources section of my website, www.happinessexperts.ca. Print it out and stick it on your fridge for quick reference.

Don't be intimidated if your diet primarily consists of group four and five foods. It's easier than you might think to make the change to the delicious foods found in groups one and two. As evidence, just look at the breakfast suggestions made earlier. Sweet and flavorful fruits, and refreshing savory vegetables are wonderful. I bake low-fat, mouthwatering yam fries. We eat scrumptious butternut squash lasagna with whole-grain pasta and low-fat cottage cheese. Today I had a delicious taco salad with corn chips, spicy salsa, spinach, cucumbers, tomatoes, yellow pepper and no-fat greek yogurt. It was awesome!

When you begin to make the switch, notice how you feel. I expect you will be more energetic, alert and cheery. I discourage calorie counting as the primary means to lose weight. There is strong evidence that reducing caloric intake results in lower metabolic rates, so you experience feelings of low energy and high deprivation with little weight loss. Instead, eat lots of group one and two foods. Avoid group four and five foods. For most people, this switch in dietary emphasis is more than enough to successfully lose weight without the feelings of deprivation that come with calorie counting.

If you grew up like I did with meat as the focal point of most meals, this switch may seem daunting. Try planning three suppertime meals per week without meat. Starting here and staying with it for a few months will show you that meatless meals are easy to prepare and delicious. Once you have formed a habit of three vegetarian suppers per week, it may be relatively easy to expand your cooking to include a couple more meatless meals. Soon enough you may find yourself barely cooking group five meats. Bit by bit, your culinary skills and your palate will make the switch to preferring the habit (the lifestyle) of healthy food. My own family still adds some meat to several suppertime meals. We like the flavor, but more importantly, I have one son who is allergic to several alternative proteins—fish, nuts, legumes and eggs. So I tend to cut a typical one-person serving of chicken into small pieces and prepare it as part of a four-serving mixed vegetable dish with whole grain pasta, quinoa or brown rice.

Body: Physical Well-Being

I want to point out an exception to the slow, but steady progression to greater health. If you are a long way from having a healthy lifestyle and are dealing with serious health risks as a result, then really there should be no alternative to switching dramatically and switching for good. If you are suffering daily from the debilitating effects of type-two diabetes, cardiovascular disease or obesity, it would be a good idea to invest heavily in changing your diet. Consider it a make-over, just like on reality TV. You are not subjecting yourself to a loss of your unhealthy self, instead you are giving yourself the gift of better health. Once you have stuck to your regime for as little as three weeks, you will not want to go back to your old diet. You will simply feel so much better.

Yum! Eat lots of plants with little or no processing (groups one and two). Have fun with spices. Avoid heavy saturated fats found mostly in animal based foods (groups four and five). Go easy on salts and sweeteners (group three). Make exceptions, but make them special by being rare and savored. Look younger, feel great, and be healthy.

TIP

Along with eating lots of the right things, try this: buy smaller dinnerware. Yes, it can be that simple. Replace your old dinnerware with smaller plates, bowls and cups. Convincing research shows two things:

1) dinnerware has grown in size during the same period when obesity became an epidemic; and

2) people fill dinnerware proportionately the same and still eat in accordance with the size of the serving.

So most of us will feel content clearing all the food on our plate regardless of the dinnerware size. Google Brian Wansink if you want to learn about his powerful research findings regarding portion control.

Points to ponder:

- What's in your pantry? Have you got lots of healthy food on hand?
- How do you feel when you know you have eaten a healthy meal?
- What three things could you do this week that would improve your food-related lifestyle?

5 Sleep, Rest and Sex

Why is sex in a chapter that also includes sleep? Perhaps it's because both typically happen in a bed. Although, I have also slept on the couch, in a car, on the floor, on grass . . . well, sex happens in all those places too. The real answer is that both can be restorative and lift our physical and mental health. Sleep is absolutely necessary and as I get older, I find that sex is less necessary and more of a luxury than I used to think. But as a rite of passage, the physical, emotional and mental quest for sex is present in us all. So let's turn to the necessity for and omnipresence of sleep, rest and sex each in turn.

Sleep

For all you readers who regularly get eight full hours of deep, refreshing slumber each night, keep doing whatever it is you do. Enjoy what you have and recognize what an enriching gift it is. For everyone else, here are some things you can learn about sleep that may help you.

Give sleep its due

Like food, water and air, you need it. I am astonished by my own past attitude about sleep. I suspect many readers can relate to my old perspective. I used to appreciate sleep only when it was just past—in the morning before getting out of bed, I savored and marveled at how good sleep felt. As well, oftentimes in the middle of the night after I have awoken, I have craved a quiet mind and a still body. I wanted to fall promptly back to sleep; so much so that I got frustrated, even angry, that my time was being wasted in bed NOT sleeping (and since my partner was a good sleeper, it was pretty darn rare that I was having sex as an alternative to sleep).

It's odd, in some respects, that I lost so many hours of desired sleep over many years and yet did not seem to care much for sleep except briefly upon awakening or manically during restless periods in the middle of the night. Would anyone reasonably go years without considering other similar physical necessities? Could I consider food only as a momentary topic of interest when I was not eating contentedly? No, our lives revolve around food and the necessity of regular nutrition. Even very busy people make plans to eat—they buy groceries, clip fast-food coupons, and often punctuate their busy lives with the ceremony of social occasions centered around food. We anticipate with some eager delight our upcoming or current relationship with food.

By contrast, sleep—an equally necessary daily part of life—is often given no consideration. It's an inconvenience and a distraction from things we would rather do. Both when life's demands are too great or when bored with inactivity, sleep is all too often a neglected—maybe even resented—necessity. When busy, we work until far past a proper bedtime. When with friends, we readily push the envelope to steal from sleep a few more minutes or even hours. And sadly, even when simple leisure time at home is present, many of us will stay up watching TV, surfing the internet or reading a book, even when we know we should be sleeping. Why do we value the necessary function of sleep so little, except when we have just awoken and crave more sleep? No one is exactly sure why.

Certainly, many people do value sleep, plan for it, and facilitate its rich experience. Unfortunately, for those who do not value sleep, the modern world readily accommodates sleep deprivation. All manner of devices allow us to distract ourselves from sleep, with the most obvious and pernicious being electrical light. You can generally avoid an early, deep slumber if you light your life up. Just a few generations ago, not many people had access to sleep-disruptive artificial light. These people didn't have to consciously value sleep so much because once it was dark, few distractions kept them awake (except perhaps sex).

Am I valuing sleep as a part of my everyday lifestyle?

The point is this: if you are a person who is not getting as much sleep as you need and want, ask yourself, "Am I valuing sleep as a part of my everyday lifestyle, or only when sleep is absent and I desperately want it?" If you are not accommodating sleep as a part of a healthy lifestyle, then it's time to learn how. Give sleep its due value.

Sleep hygiene

Researchers and practical experience tell us there are numerous behaviors that encourage and facilitate healthy sleep patterns. (Poor emotional health can lead to lost sleep. This will be addressed later in the book). Behaviors that help with sleep are:

- Exercise every day. Moving your body reduces stress and assists with signaling the brain to induce sleep. Sleep, of course, facilitates restoration of our physical bodies. Daily exercise doesn't have to be intense and drawn out. An after-supper walk for 20-30 minutes is reasonable. Do not, however, engage in vigorous exercise within an hour or two of bedtime. Your adrenaline will still be pumping through your veins, keeping you wide awake.

- Reduce exposure to bright lights from electronic devices (TVs, tablets, smartphones, etc.) in the 30 minutes before bed. These artificial lights are intense and contain color elements that mimic daytime sunshine. Instead, give yourself the pleasure of a relaxing activity with dim lighting: read a book, take a bath, knit, talk with your spouse, or engage in some other calming hobby.

- Keep snacks light within an hour of bedtime. Eating and drinking stimulate the digestive system, which is a major power draw for our heart. The practical mechanics of processing food is an activity suited for awake time. Everyone varies in their tolerance, but for most of us only a light snack can be consumed without risking wakefulness.

- Avoid work or other demanding tasks in the hour before bed. Whether it's a report being drafted or an important discussion about raising your kids, try to avoid these activities right before bed. Be conscious of the value you place on sleep. Respect the need to wind yourself down.

- Stick to regular routines, including going to bed at the same time each night and keeping your bedroom free of stimulation. Make sure your brain associates your bed with sleep (and perhaps sex) only. Do not regularly eat, watch TV, or do other hobbies in bed. Make the room dark and quiet. Wear earplugs if necessary. Shift workers face a special challenge with this aspect of sleep hygiene. The perils of shift work are well known. Not having regular biological patterns is harmful to one's health. Shift workers live shorter lives and suffer higher rates of substance abuse and depression. If you are a shift worker, lean more heavily into the other recommendations besides the regular bedtimes.

- Count your blessings. As you settle into your bed, turn your mind to the blessings in your life. You may have all kinds of demands to consider as you lay in bed, but worrying and planning are negative and are almost always stimulating. Instead, turn your mind to the positive attributes of your day or your life in general. It may feel artificial at first, but you may be surprised how quickly you habituate to this bedtime routine. Positive reflections will help you to relax and fall asleep.

First and Second Waking

Many people do not struggle to fall asleep. Their issue is staying asleep. Typically, people with this complaint will wake four or five hours after they went to bed. And, like me, they will be unable to fall back to sleep quickly. Often, they will get up and go to the bathroom and then find they feel too alert for sleep.

If this sounds familiar, you may also know about the frustration (even despair) that accompanies this sleeplessness. I used to get quite worked up about being awake, such that my chances of actually going back to sleep completely vanished. Fortunately, there is a potent cure for most people with this problem. Little known to modern people, we aren't actually supposed to sleep in one long seven or eight hour stretch—hurray for those who do—but if you are routinely awake at three or four in the morning, the following information could change your life.

People who lived before electricity did not sleep through the night. Sleep scientists have uncovered ample evidence of this. No, they could not interview our ancestors or detect past behavior patterns for 3:30 a.m. But they did uncover relevant historical writing with consistent references to wakeful periods in the night.

These references were not the tormented voice of writers who could not sleep. Rather, the records show that, in common parlance, historical people understood the concept of one or two regular periods of wakefulness that interrupted the night's sleep. It was so common that people had terms to describe these periods.

In English, there was "first waking", which described the one-to-two hours in the night during which almost all adults were awake. "Second Waking" was the quiet, lovely wakefulness that is typical before a person gets up for the day.

"First Waking" is shown from the literature in many cultures to be a routine time for pleasant activities. During this period of wakefulness people had sex, prayed and contemplated spiritual pursuits, and even visited neighbors. Without electric light, the activities they could do were limited in terms of how productive they could be. So, without resentment for being awake, they used the time of First Waking for pleasurable, enriching experiences.

In our modern world, we have industrialized our behavior to conform with society's expectations. These expectations are entirely dictated by the irrelevance of sunlight. With artificial light, there are no reasons that all workers cannot promptly attend their paid employment by 8:30 or 9:00 a.m. They will go home and participate in activity with their family and friends from roughly 5:00 to 10:30 p.m, at which time they will turn off the lights and sleep. Industry may want this from us, but many people remain attuned to our natural, ancestral rhythms, which are a function of the sun's expressions of the days and seasons.

Equatorial people, whom we all have as our forebears, had roughly 12 hours of sunlight and 12 hours of darkness every day. They did not sleep for twelve consecutive hours. Rather, they had First and Second Wakings that were natural, gentle and attuned to their well-being.

If you wake after four or five hours of sleep, you are like the 5,000 human generations that came before you. Pause and deeply consider this for a moment. Waking up for more than one hour in the middle of the night is completely normal. It is doing no harm to you. It is not inconvenient or bad. In fact, it is an opportunity to do something good for yourself. Accept reality. You are awake. Do something gentle such as writing, reading, or, my favorite, listening to podcasts.

Since I came to understand my reality of a First and Second Waking, I have learned to not only accept it, but also use that time to pursue my own wellness. I used to write upon First Waking. However, the writing itself was often too stimulating and I wanted bright light as I wrote. This tended to inhibit, on some occasions, going back to sleep. I am now in a multi-year habit of listening to recordings during First Waking. I simply press play on the recording I selected before I first went to bed. In general, I have chosen enriching non-fiction audio recordings, most recently focusing on spiritual and psychological teachings from the Eastern traditions. Most nights, I am back to sleep in a little less than an hour. To accommodate this period of wakefulness, I try to be in bed by 10 p.m. and I get up a little past 6 a.m. I get a pretty regular seven-hour sleep and I feel great. It took me nearly 30 years to figure this pattern out.

It's worth noting that, even with good sleep habits, you may still face the odd night of poor sleep. I have experienced nights when I had more than one waking or had difficulty returning to sleep despite following my prescriptions before bed. It happens. The most important thing is to find a system that works for you most of the time.

Find the First Waking activity that suits you best: have an electronic device read something to you, get up and read or write under gentle light, meditate or do very light, relaxing yoga, or knit. Whatever it is you choose to do, make sure it provides for a few of these comforts:

- Warm — being cold will make your return to sleep difficult.

- Enjoyable — Unpleasant tasks will leave you tense.

- Minimal artificial light — particularly compact florescent lights (CFL), which mimic the stimulating light of the sun. The same is true for all screens on phones, tablets, TVs and computers.

- Accommodate for First Waking in your daily schedule. Plan to be awake for an hour, which means getting to bed one hour earlier.

Sleep is wonderful. A deep, restful sleep improves every aspect of our lives. It makes us mentally sharp, physically stronger and emotionally more resilient. You devalue sleep if you behave in a way that discourages regular, good quality slumber. If reading this is setting off some alarm bells in you, then attention to sleep may be an essential component to improving your happiness and overall quality of life.

Rest

Is there any down time in your day? More specifically, is there down time in your mid-to-late afternoon? If your only rest period is in the few minutes or one to two hours before bed, you could likely benefit from a bit more relaxation and rejuvenation.

In the animal kingdom nearly all mammals nap. Some nap a lot. All our primate cousins nap. In an ideal world we would all nap too. However, most of us stop napping when we are about three years old. If naps ever resume, it's often not until we are senior citizens. This is a shame because a short nap is an excellent, restorative mental and physical restart. It's like rebooting your computer and seeing it perform at its best.

For many readers, perhaps napping is out of the question. Most working people don't have a time, a place or adequate peace to nap. So be it. Can you see alternatives to napping that would give you a few minutes of relief from the pressures and demands of your busy day?

I had a client a few years back—let's call her Linda—who, for many years, never took breaks at work. We saw this as one thing to work on to create more work-life balance. Linda resolved that she would not eat lunch at her desk. With only a few exceptions each year, she kept her resolution. Of course, there is nothing that makes eating lunch at one's desk bad. For Linda, it was the failure to rest that was the issue. For the 10 years prior to her resolution, she always ate at her desk so she could continue her "very important" work. But by breaking for lunch, she literally got new perspective on her work. Linda realized the world carried on just fine without her while she ate her lunch. She lost some of her self-importance and that alone was a huge burden off her shoulders. As well, by breaking for lunch, she allowed her mind to think of things other than work. When she wasn't thinking about work, her subconscious often sprang forward with solutions to work problems. Often, she walked or played ping pong during her lunch break. For a few years, it was convenient for her to zip home and have lunch with her spouse and her kids, who were homeschooled. This was a delightful, brief social connection with the people she most loved.

We all deserve and greatly benefit from a temporary escape from the busyness that fills a typical work day. Lunch and coffee breaks are good things. Take advantage of them for a true break away from your work tasks. In addition, use your commute time for rewarding tasks like reading a book or listening to an audiobook. Fit yoga or squash or some other enjoyable exercise in your day.

Simplistic? Yes, but all work and no play makes Jack and Jane dull people. As well, it risks exhausting people's mental and physical resources. I have worked with many clients who take tremendous pride in their work. Too often, unfortunately, they lack balance and perspective on this part of their lives. A little rest goes a long, long way.

Sex

I am not Dr. Ruth or a sex athlete. My advice here is relatively simple and straightforward. Sex and the quest to have it are natural, normal parts of life. Orgasm triggers pleasure centers in the brain that are acutely powerful. In part, these pleasure centers are the same ones triggered when you use cocaine. This is why romantic love—when couples often behave like hyperactive bunnies—is so wonderful. The couple is experiencing potent cocaine-like highs regularly. This stage of a relationship often lacks sound judgement and measured, rational behaviors. So on the one hand, sex is awesome and makes us feel good. On the other hand, obsessive pursuit of sex is often harmful.

So what is the prescription? Have sex often, perhaps even once a day if you and your partner are into it. Don't deny yourself this need. And if you have no partner, enjoy pleasuring yourself. With moderation, sex—including by yourself—is fine. In fact, it's more than fine. Sex has substantial benefits, including:

- Boosting your immune system, so you can fight off disease.
- Lowering your blood pressure.
- Adding to your overall quantity of physical exercise.
- Keeping hormones in balance, which has many benefits including better pain tolerance and better sleep.
- Reducing the risk of prostate cancer in men.
- Reducing stress.
- Increasing commitment and attachment for couples.
- It's pleasurable and fun.

We all know, however that sometimes sex can spell trouble. Sex that is exploitive, uncontrollably compulsive, violent or hurtful to others is over the line. So, too, is sex that is unprotected in non-monogamous, uncommitted relationships. Disease and heartache can usurp any benefits of sex.

Sex is so powerful—with such terrific physical pleasures and hormonal surges—that its pursuit can become compulsive. Sex addiction may seem trite or a fictional disease; however, excessive sex (including masturbation) is, in my view, harmful. Like any other overindulgent behavior, it has negative consequences, both psychically and physically. Time, energy and one's consciousness can get tied up in pursuing sexual gratification. If sex is a distraction from things that would truly bring benefit, it is happening too much. Mastering your urge to have sex is basic to being a mature person. Frequent masturbation often comes with compulsive porn viewing (particularly for men). This activity, when uncontrolled, devalues sex. It removes all the better aspects of sex with other humans—love, intrigue, romance, generosity and kindness. Moreover, it eliminates femininity and masculinity and leaves the viewer with bodies and their parts. Objectifying men or women is contrary to anyone's interests.

Short of the aforementioned problematic situations, sex is good. Western and eastern cultures alike often have a lot of unhappy-making hang-ups with sex. Noting the precautions, I would encourage readers to let go of the views that have come from religious or other dogmatic belief systems. Be a good person and appreciate sex as a relatively basic physical need like food and sleep. Enjoy it!

Points to ponder:

- How is your sleep hygiene? Are you valuing sleep? What could you start doing (or stop doing) to facilitate better sleep habits?

- In what way do you rest during the middle of the day? What would be ideal? How can you move towards an ideal pattern of rest?

- What are your hang-ups with sex? In what ways could you counter any negative messages you have learned about sex?

- What conversation with your partner might enhance the quality and frequency of your sex life?

6 Disease and Aging

The human fate is to grow old, get sick and die. I fully accept this fact. I do not waste any time wishing otherwise.

Although every individual birthday is of no real significance to me, cumulatively I most definitely am not the man I was 25 years ago. I use reading glasses. I have a bald spot. I have a growing inventory of wrinkles. My muscles ache and injuries recover much slower than they used to. That said, I weigh the same as I did 25 years ago and because I run and cycle regularly my cardiovascular fitness is about the same as it was then too. All in all I am almost as physically capable as I ever was and my physical decline is modest. There is no reason for me to expect anything too much different in the next 25 years.

This is a critical point: as a fit and healthy middle-aged man, I expect my aging will result in a gradual and modest decline. Perhaps the following graph (Fig. 1) represents my past and expected future:

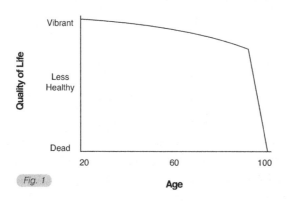

Fig. 1

This is the projected trajectory for anyone who is fit and healthy. I was vibrant and healthy at 20 years old, then I experienced modest decline that can be expected to continue trending modestly downward, until one day I drop dead. I think many people imagine a much more discouraging decline with age. People may expect there is a steady and precipitous decline that ends in death, like this (Fig. 2):

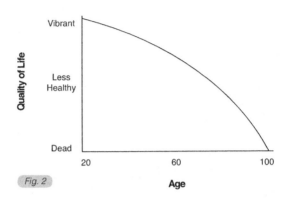

Fig. 2

I am sorry to say that if you are looking at this graph and you place your own age and vitality at a similar location on the graph, your future may be bleaker than what is shown. When people have poor fitness and health in middle age, their risk of premature death is greater. Let's take, for example, a 45-year-old male who is obese, drug dependent for type-2 diabetes, and at significant risk of progressive cardiovascular disease. His graph may look like this (Fig. 3):

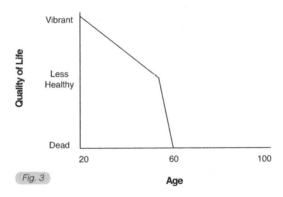

Fig. 3

Cardiovascular disease, obesity and type-2 diabetes are serious conditions. Without correction and some reversal, early death is likely. Sadly, we all know people who passed away in their late 50s or early 60s because they simply carried too many risk factors for ill health and early death.

Some of us may have no lifestyle concerns that would lead to this outcome, but fate may take us early. For example, a fit and healthy 55-year-old may develop terminal cancer. Death at 58 may be his or her fate in spite of an absence of known lifestyle risk factors. This is bad luck, for sure. Their graph may look like this (Fig. 4):

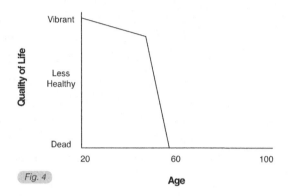

Fig. 4

As you can see, even in this gloomy scenario, the quality of life for the cancer victim (Fig. 4) is infinitely superior relative to the person with chronic lifestyle diseases (Figure 3). While the cancer victim died too young, he or she had a very good ride up to that point. Before then, due to underlying good health and fitness, many benefits existed:

- Played sports
- Had good sex
- Looked nice
- Felt energetic
- Recovered well from aches and injuries
- Was confident about the body's abilities
- Maintained mental sharpness

By contrast, a sick lifestyle leads to a sick life: limited activity, low libido and erectile dysfunction, unattractiveness, lethargy, and discouragement or depression due to one's physical condition.

This illustration of how we age has been loosely adapted from the work of Dr. Henry Lodge. He is a medical doctor who counsels sustained healthy lifestyles

Get fit, stay fit, eat healthy food and you can expect the best.

so as to increase the odds of a long, healthy life. He co-wrote the somewhat light-hearted book, *Younger Next Year*, about the serious subject of health. The premise of the work is that quality of life and age at death is, on average, more affected by our way of living than fateful occurrences. Get fit, stay fit, eat healthy food and you can expect the best. Chances are you'll be physically capable right up to your mid-80s or even into your 90s (depending on your genetic predisposition). Don't we all wish for this? I want to be healthy, active and of right mind until I am in my late 90s. Then, the day after my 100th birthday it will be fine with me if I drop dead of a heart attack. I certainly wouldn't want to ruin the party by dying on the day of my birthday.

Notably, Dr. Lodge's work is all about coming back from middle-age risk factors to healthy, low-risk states of being. Read his book for a detailed description to find out if you are running the risk of premature death and a diminished quality of life. The two chapters in this book on fitness and nutrition are all about avoiding this fate that, tragically, is shared by so many people in our modern world.

Only a minority of people experience chronic disease unrelated to their lifestyle. Diseases such as Crohn's, multiple sclerosis and type-1 diabetes have nothing to do with the lifestyles of those who fall victim to them. However, a large part of managing these and similar diseases does fall to lifestyle. Coping, resiliency and slowing disease progression are often substantially improved with a conscientious commitment to safely maximizing fitness and good nutrition.

It's out of the scope of this book to advise on any specific disease, but there is always a place for fitness and nutrition to be a central component in a clinical care plan. If you are dealing with a chronic disease, speak to your health care professional(s) about maximizing your quality of life. High quality nutrition and appropriate fitness objectives are certain to improve quality of life and to provide a measure of control over your own body. This can be a satisfying contributor to good mental health, even in the face of chronic disease.

We all get older, eventually get sick and die. I want to get older with minimal decline in physical or mental function. I wish the same for you. Good nutrition and fitness not only boost the immune system to reduce the risk of contracting disease, they also ameliorate many diseases' degree of disability.

How do you make the journey back—or for the first time—to good health? Oftentimes, the "how" of being healthy is relatively well understood. It's mostly common sense. Even when there are gaps in knowledge, books, coaches, doctors and others will have helpful and unhelpful advice for you. It is relatively rare for the challenge to lie in "how" to be healthy. The real opportunity exists in the "why" to be healthy. I hope this chapter has stimulated some thoughts about why good health facilitates a happy, high-quality and long life. Perhaps you may benefit from some reflections on your own "why".

Points to Ponder:

- Consider the people you love. What will it take for you to be all you can be to your children and their children? What would you like your senior years to be like? What will your spouse need and want from you? What gifts do you need to still share with the world? Think these questions through. Write down a few notes. Make your mental images vivid. Imagine your yet-to-be-born grandson's graduation. How old will you be? What level of activity can you envision? What would it take for you to maximize your well-being? Set a big picture goal for yourself. If you are 40, ask yourself what you will be like when you are 55? Envision your best self.

- In detail, list three near-term, realistic activities you can commit to in the next seven days. When will you do them? What do you need to prepare in order to do them? Write it down. Put your promise to yourself on your bathroom mirror.

7 Money

We need things. Most of us really like and want more things. There is a world of difference between what we want and what we need. This chapter explores the difference between the two.

Fortunately, you don't have to rely on my opinion of what constitutes a need or a want. Scientists have given a lot of consideration to these concerns. There are basic biological needs and there are psychological needs. The biological context is easy to understand. For all of pre-history, our ancestors lived in tribal settings where life's daily pursuits were mostly about getting our biological needs met: shelter from the elements, sufficient calories and fresh water, basic clothing for warmth, and some knowledge and application of healing methods in the event of an injury or sickness. Nothing has changed. That's still all any of us really needs. However, from a psycho-social perspective, we require more than just the barest of survival needs met. We also need to fit in and belong to a community, and we need some level of security regarding our future. We need to know that not just today's biological needs are met, but that tomorrow's and next month's provisions will be there too.

What is the extent of this psycho-social need? It seems insatiable. We are surrounded by excess and greed. We see grotesque wealth in the hands of the few. We see overconsumption of all kinds. From obesity to 100-inch TV screens. From super-size fries to million dollar sports trading cards. From unrealistically large breast implants to fatal customer stampedes at discount stores. We live in a culture where more is better. And regardless of income level, ethnicity, political views or religion, most of us are inclined the same way. It's as if we all live by this mantra: "My mission is to earn and consume as much as I can in the time I've got." Some folks are very successful in this game of acquiring things and some not so much. Intuitively, we would think that those few who made their millions and live a life of luxury would be over-the-moon happy and the folks who only achieved moderate middle class lifestyles would be disappointed.

Strikingly, this conclusion is wrong. The rich are not proportionately happier than the middle class. Some excellent research has been done on this point. Nobel Prize winning economist Daniel Kahneman teamed up with psychologist Angus Deaton and published a fascinating study in 2010. The study surveyed 450,000 people. Among other things, the researchers gathered data about people's day-to-day happiness and their household income. What the study concluded is fascinating. Household incomes below $75,000 USD per year were associated with less happiness. Households earning $75,000 or more were happier than the "poorer" households. However, households earning more than $75,000 (sometimes much more) had no greater day-to-day happiness. There is a beautiful and perfectly reasonable explanation for this. When a person is poor and the ability to meet basic biological needs is insecure, he is less happy. When someone enjoys a household income of $75,000, he not only has his biological needs met today, but is generally confident that the mortgage payment and next week's groceries are all taken care of as well. Biological needs are secure. A person can then turn his mind to pursuits beyond meeting basic biological needs. He can pursue meaningful personal relationships, hobbies, spiritual goals, good physical health...whatever. But if a person earns $500,000 per year, her basic biological needs are not met any more completely than those earning $75,000 per year. Thus, she cannot/does not enjoy any greater day-to-day happiness.

Is $75,000 a magic number? No. The study was from a few years ago. Go ahead and add an inflation adjustment. Add or subtract a few thousand dollars if you are in a low-cost or high-cost city. Or make a genuine commitment to simpler living and subtract several more thousand dollars. Convert US dollars to whatever your currency is. All of this doesn't matter much except to say you need to contemplate deeply your own biological security. If your studied observation is that your household's earning power is sufficient to meet biological needs plus a little more for added security, then you can stop worrying about and striving for more. By contrast, if your biological needs are insecurely met, your focus should be on changing your circumstances. Move to where good jobs are plentiful, get training for a better job, find a compatible partner to share living expenses with (remember, it's about household income), learn to live simply in a smaller house with fewer things, buy secondhand goods, cook your own meals instead of eating out.

In addition to these strategies, consider this: it's all in our heads. I've met wonderfully happy poor people whose day-to-day enjoyment is not significantly impacted by concerns for tomorrow's biological needs. There are also countless stories of exceedingly rich people who live emotionally desperate lives. If your circumstances are tough, get real, devise a plan to make them better and then work your plan. Don't, however, deny your ability to be happy as you step-by-step change your life for the better.

Some readers may think this advice is unrealistic or maybe even unkind. Perhaps it seems to have too little regard for the struggle and great stress of getting by in poverty. Consider another aspect of the study done by Kahneman and Deaton. In addition to happiness and income, they asked respondents about the levels of stress in their day-to-day lives. Many of the "wealthy" respondents reported a lot of day-to-day stress. The wealthiest were particularly likely to report high levels of stress. Managing all their possessions and high-paying enterprises took a lot out of them.

I don't want to suggest that their type of stress is comparable or worse than the stress that comes from deprivation. When healthcare and housing are low quality and food supply is tenuous, there is a profound and very challenging kind of stress. I know I would be unhappy in this circumstance. Yet I know happiness is possible even in dire poverty. Monks and nuns often choose poverty and yet live very happy lives. International surveys show surprising levels of happiness in very poor countries. Mexico, for one, seems to compensate for poverty with closer family relations and a carefree attitude. Mexico consistently ranks higher than the United States and several other much richer nations on surveys of perceived happiness.

I have experienced the findings of Kahneman and Deaton's study in my own life. My dad died of cancer when I was two, leaving behind my stay-at-home mom with six children ages two to 10. My dad had been a high school teacher. His earnings were just sufficient to support our family of eight people. When he died, there was a modest life insurance payment. There was no regular income and a mortgage on a big house that had just been bought for our sizeable family. My mom did not return to her low-paying teaching job until I was in kindergarten three years later.

My memories of my childhood are mostly happy. I never worried whether there would be enough food to eat. Ignorant bliss, perhaps. As I got older I started to realize more and more that we were not well off compared to some other families. I rarely had a bike that fit me and invariably it was a hand-me-down from an older sibling. My clothes were similarly well-worn. None of my friends drank powdered skim milk, but we did. When I grew to be a teenager and was suddenly self-conscious about my appearance my mom made it seem effortless that she could afford to buy current, fashionable clothes for me instead of hand-me-downs. I expect I will never have a great insight into how many sacrifices she made for me and my brothers and sisters. I can only get a sense of it from my own loving (and mostly joyful) service to my sons.

As was expected of me, I went off to university, which was paid for mostly through student loans and working part-time jobs. When I left university, I had expectations for very modest earnings. I don't know why I had those expectations, but I guess I had never known anything different. Moreover, my Bachelor of Arts degree with a major in Political Science did not make me the hottest employment prospect.

With the exception of my university years, my adult life has been the financial opposite of my childhood. My Bachelor of Arts degree with a major in Political Science led to well paid work almost right away. By age 28 I was hired into a high paying executive role and I envisioned a road of success before me—vice president by 40, big house, two cars, vacations in the sun . . . the whole deal. After a short time, though, I realized I had zero ambition to climb the corporate ladder. I knew a higher income would not make me happier and would, in fact, reduce my time with my spouse and my son, who brought me immense happiness.

I chose more happiness. My position (and the similar ones that followed) paid enough money to provide for my family and invest in our future financial well-being. Looking back, I feel fortunate to have recognized that acquiring more would not add to my happiness.

When I left the organization two years ago to teach, write and coach full-time, it was difficult to bid adieu to the guaranteed paycheck. My inconsistent entrepreneur's income would certainly be less than I was used to. But I knew I could live happily with far less money.

I tell this story so some readers may feel inspired. Yes, you need to earn enough money to meet your biological needs and a little bit more. Yet, we don't need to engage in the race to attain more, more, more because more stuff will not give you more day-to-day happiness.

Figure out what amount—perhaps in the loose ball-park of $75,000—your family needs to earn. Then do what you can to approach that mark. If you reach it or surpass it, please then grant yourself the tremendous freedom to recognize the state of "enough". With that freedom firmly felt and understood, you can choose what to do. That could even be earning a lot more money for the joy of the endeavor rather than the mirage of necessity.

Points to ponder:

- To what degree are you secure in your basic biological needs of food, shelter, and clothing?

- In what ways could simplifying your life make you more secure?

8 Safety and Security

Have you ever heard of a lottery winner who, a short time after winning millions of dollars, grew deeply indebted and had to declare bankruptcy? Sadly it is a well-known story.

What about the young sports star who earned millions in salary and endorsements only to end up destitute after his career has ended?

Have you read about a tragic death of an innocent young man who lived in the ghetto? All too often the victim has eschewed the gang lifestyle, yet was in the wrong place at the wrong time and lost his life due to an errant bullet intended for someone else.

Can you remember a story of an extreme athlete who lost the use of his limbs in a terrible sporting accident? He pushed the limits of his sport and, in a moment, life changed permanently with severe consequences.

I expect your life is probably very different from that of a lottery winner, a rich sports star, a young man in the ghetto or an extreme athlete. Based on demographic data collected about people who read personal development books like this, you are likely between the ages 25 and 55, middle class with an education beyond high school and have already met with a high degree of life success. You probably know your actions can result in good things and so you continue to look for good paths. You are genuinely curious about how to live your best possible life.

In other words, you are not a lottery winner, sports star, inner city youth or extreme athlete. But, like them, you can experience downfalls in your life. It's possible that, in spite of your positive life and aspiration for even greater things, you too could experience poor financial planning and bankruptcy or take avoidable risks to your personal safety.

If you want to be sure you are attending to basic preservation of life, limb and financial security, then settle in for a few more pages.

Security

Twenty years working for a large organization has given me a substantial defined benefit pension plan. The plan is in excellent financial health according to independent actuaries. Leaving my paid employment to start my own business and write a book was much less risky knowing that I will be eligible to collect a modest but sufficient pension at age 55.

In addition, since my income for many years exceeded the "magic" $75,000 mark, I spent the "excess" money on assets. I define assets as things you can own that you have good reason to believe will hold or increase their value over the long run. The assets I bought were primarily real estate. Although I don't come from a wealthy family, I managed to buy five properties with a total of nine distinct residential units. My former spouse and I generally bought properties for which the rent we could collect would exceed the expenses required to own and operate them. We are hardly tycoons. But after many years, the rent now sufficiently exceeds expenses to give us a modest monthly income. In another 10 years, when we may want to be fully retired, I expect the net income will be greater still. Of course, there are no guarantees, but barring major economic collapse, our pensions and rental incomes should permit us to live comfortably in the later years of our lives.

If you want this kind of financial security, buy assets. Give priority to this task. Make it important—even sacrifice for it. In spite of temporary and fully expected fluctuations in markets, your assets will, in the long run, be worth more than what you paid for them. Just remember to do your calculations so you can be reasonably sure that the income from your asset will be more than the costs to own it.

Can you distinguish between a possession and an investment? Will your car increase in value over the long run? What about a speed boat or scuba diving gear? These are not assets. All of them—noting some very rare exceptions of collector's items kept in mint condition—will become worthless over the long run. When your financial planner or banker includes these items in your net worth, he or she is deluding you. A fancy car, showy boat or other things we buy and later dispose of are not real assets. Real assets, over the long run, at minimum hold their value and have a reasonable likelihood of gaining value. Usually, over 15 to 30 years, a significant gain can be expected. Assets are real estate, many stocks and bonds, and a few other select physical items like gold, silver, and—for people with genuine expertise—art and collectibles. Assets often require on-going diligent care. My real estate holdings require about six hours of attention each month.

Many readers may still feel the sting of the 2008/2009 Great Recession. Some parts of the U.S. and other parts of the world are still recovering from the financial collapse that many assets suffered. However, most mainstream asset classes have recovered—stock markets rebounded—and in most marketplaces, house prices are back to their 2006 levels (the housing bubble burst in 2007). So in spite of the devastating consequences of the recent recession, asset values have done what asset values regularly do—they went up over the long run. Be a long run investor. Even if you are a high risk entrepreneur, I recommend you also buy long run assets. Your future security and peace of mind will be forever grateful.

When I bought properties, I mostly used equity in our personal home as down payments for the rental properties. Every time I increased my debt, I had reasonable confidence that the debt payment would always be paid by my tenants. Having been a small-scale landlord for over 20 years now, this belief has never been wrong. Debt is not an enemy. It is simply a vehicle. You can drive it to a party on the strip, have a great time and wake up with a hangover in the morning —think consumer debt for cars, vacations and personal housing that goes well beyond your needs. Or you can drive the debt vehicle to conservative locations like student loans, blue chip stocks and quality rental properties. The difference between good debt and bad debt is this: will the item you bought with your debt pay you back? Most likely your student loan will. Your quality stock will. Your rental property will. However, your car, your big screen TV and your all-inclusive vacation in Jamaica will not pay you back.

Buy quality, long run assets.

Buy quality, long run assets.

This prescription perhaps doesn't sound easy and it's not. If it were easy, our culture would not be awash in consumer debt. To live a happy, balanced life you will have to swim upstream. When we choose to avoid this kind of debt, our mammalian brains cry out because we want instant gratification from pleasurable experiences. Our more evolved primate brains need to be in charge, thinking about and acting in our long-run best interests.

If your primate, rational brain sometimes loses the contest of wills with your impulsive more primitive self, be kind to yourself as you reflect on it. We're all vulnerable to our more base instincts. We all make mistakes. Life is about what we learn from them and how we act going forward.

If financial security is an area of concern for you, you may need more help than this short chapter can offer. Make an appointment with a financial planner and/or a debt counselor. In the meantime, here are a few useful tips that make a real difference for many people:

- Freeze your credit card in a block of ice. You can melt the ice in a genuine emergency; it never comes out on an impulse.

- Automate your bad debt payments so you make the maximum payment you can afford from each of your paychecks. If you get paid bi-weekly, then make debt payments bi-weekly even if the debt only requires a monthly payment.

- Carry only $20 in cash.

- Write down where every penny you spend goes. Awareness of your spending is the beginning of insight and remedial action.

- Make an investment plan. Start young and don't stop until the day you retire.

It isn't all sacrifices, hard discipline, scrimping and saving. It's bit by bit, regular exercise of control over your own life. The rewards are enormous over the long run.

Safety

In my 14 years in the disability management business I met dozens, if not hundreds, of people who wished they could redo five seconds of their lives. On-the-job injuries are rarely a result of freak accidents. Instead, a series of causes—many of which foretold what would happen—led to catastrophic consequences. These causes invariably had human errors or lapses in judgment associated with them. Sometimes the error arose from people far removed and safe from the danger that others became exposed to. Other times the injured person was primarily or entirely responsible for what befell them. In nearly every case, the beaten and broken bodies resulted from completely preventable events.

We can all experience momentary distractions with tragic consequences. This brief section on safety is not to wag a finger at anyone. It serves to remind us that as we pursue our best selves, we need to stay vigilant about what's important. While many of us are quick to prioritize other aspects of healthy living such as nutrition, exercise and social relationships, we often ignore personal safety. This tendency can take many forms.

My past work experience, for a brief period, included the oversight of staff who determined if an injury was eligible for workers' compensation benefits. I remember quite distinctly an occasion when an adjudicator brought to me a fact pattern she felt stretched all credibility. She simply could not believe anyone could be so foolish. A middle-aged gardener claimed a serious laceration occurred as he fell while holding a running chain saw. Perhaps this was not so unusual except for this: the worker said he was on the top step of a six-foot ladder as he was pruning a tree. The ladder toppled over on the uneven ground, bringing the gardener and his running chain saw down. No one, my adjudicator insisted, would be so stupid to work from the top step of a ladder. This is a cardinal violation of ladder safety. No one would ever climb to the top step, particularly with the surface beneath them being uneven, soft soil, she said. And she felt it well beyond believability when the gardener claimed he did this with a running chain saw. At the time I heard the story, I was about 30-years-old. I sat in awkward silence as the adjudicator waited for me to share her incredulous dismissal of the man's claim. I swallowed hard and explained to her that her injured worker was, sadly, entirely believable to me. On the past weekend I was pruning some old apple trees. I had been using a stepladder to take off some top branches and as I stood on the top step with my running chain saw, I knew that what I was doing was incredibly stupid.

As someone in the health and safety business, I can't tell you how many times I awoke in the midst of an activity to witness myself up to no good. My employer had a no cell phone use in the car policy. I drove a lot for work. And you know exactly what I let myself do time and again. Even though the choice should be easy, it takes willpower to resist the urge to use the phone in the car.

I play paintball and the possession of a captured flag in hand has been known to cause me to lose all rationality as I have dived for cover at full speed over barriers when I had no idea what was on the other side.

I have been a fool and I will likely do foolish, risky things in the future. But the trajectory in my life is to do fewer foolish things as I get older. I am sure conservatism is a normal function of aging, but I have also made deliberate choices about what I want from life. Foolish injury or general risk taking is not what I need or want.

How about you?

Do you get drunk or stoned? Your risk of death, injury, unsafe sex, involvement with police, and behaving like a boor increases exponentially.

Do you use your handheld tech gadgets while driving? Not only have you heard all the warnings, but most likely you have also experienced the frightening near misses and close calls when your attention diverts away from the activity of driving.

Do you play high-risk sports? Enjoy them, but be sure you are thinking it through. Where's the limit? What are you willing to risk for a brief thrill?

Do you live in an unsafe neighborhood? If you cannot move, how do you make yourself less likely to be victimized?

Are you in a high-risk occupation? Not only physical jobs are high risk. Are you working in a depressed or extremely stressful environment? What toll is this taking? Are there better alternatives?

Are you eating badly? Do you drive too fast? Are you gambling? Do you smoke? Are you chronically underslept? What is putting you at risk?

Finger wagging and verbal scolding is unlikely to sway any of us. Sometimes being aware of our truest, most important goals is what it takes to persuade us to avoid unnecessary risk.

Points to Ponder:

If you need motivation try this exercise:

Imagine you are turning 75 years old. You are healthy and vibrant. You are so happy to be right where you are. Your life has gone according to your plans. You are accomplished in your career, your relationships, your services to your community, and you remain sharp and mentally agile. You deserve to have pride in your beautiful life. Now imagine you are at your birthday party. Many happy people have gathered to celebrate. There is warmth and much love in the room.

It is for you. Your spouse, children and grandchildren are there. Friends and colleagues who shared in your accomplishments are also in attendance. Look around and see the smiling, friendly faces. Some of these kind-hearted people are taking turns saying just a few words about you. They are saying why they are grateful for your presence in their lives. They are saying what aspects of your character they admire. They are listing some of your most important accomplishments. Now grab a piece of paper and write down what these loving people are saying. Take your time and give this exercise its due. Savor the pleasure you deserve as you imagine this event.

Next, ask yourself if those kind words and beautiful feelings at your 75th birthday party are worth taking care of yourself for? They depend on you loving your physical self.

Before we move onto the next section of the book, I want to reflect back on what we covered in Chapter 2. We examined the concept of flow, which is a principal mechanism for increasing happiness. Flow is any activity into which you can lose yourself, applying focused concentration on the use of skills that meet a sufficient challenge. When we are in a state of flow, we tend to lose track of time and diligently engage exclusively in the task at hand. Flow can be found in all kinds of engagements—sports, cooking, playing games, research, building things, planning, etc. Invariably, these flow activities resemble work, paid or otherwise. They require your concentrated attention and a sense of genuine mastery over some worthwhile challenge. Your physical wellbeing as described in the last six chapters has infinite varieties of flow opportunities.

Your path to a happy future is not a passive one. You are called to engage in a planned pursuit of wellness. With conviction in your heart and a determined and steady application of what you have learned, not only will you master your physical domain—your body—but you will tap into the flow of happiness.

To eat well, to exercise, to earn a living, to feel safe and secure, to rest and relax are all worthy in and of themselves. Beautifully, their pursuit can be worthy simply for the joy of their engagement. In each of these past chapters, there are specific flow activities for you. Look for them, seize them, and the physical world will be your playground.

PART TWO

Mind: Mental and Emotional Happiness

This section of the book examines mind, including both mental stimulation and emotional well-being.

Regard for our mental stimulation and learning is every bit as important to our happiness as our physical health. In fact, for a time, we could ignore our physical needs and get all our satisfaction from mental pursuits. Of course, this couldn't be sustained for long; for example, the desire to eat becomes pretty compelling after just a short period of fasting. However, when our mental engagement is piqued, skipping a meal is painless (although arguably ill-advised).

The first four chapters in this section will elaborate on the necessary components of our mental well-being:

- Continuous learning, challenge and growth
- Discipline and ambition
- Creativity and curiosity
- Critical thinking, including self-evaluation

With the cultivation of mental well-being, our lives are made rich. This path is attainable for all of us. It isn't a matter of high intellect or boundless time for study; rather, it's a perspective—a way of looking at our world—that we willingly engage as we carry on in our usual activities. Our mental well-being is achieved, most often, through the acts of ordinary daily living. Every person has what it takes to achieve happiness in this area of life.

Part Two of this book not only examines the mind, but also includes a thorough consideration of how our emotional lives are central to our sense of well-being. When we are doing well in the three domains of our lives, we benefit only when it translates into positive emotions. So, for example, if your conscientious eating habits and regular exercise have resulted in you having a fit body, it is of little meaning to you if your emotional state is depressed, particularly if you find no joy in your fitness and nutrition activities. The same can be said of mental and spiritual wellness. If you are doing the right things for yourself mentally and spiritually, but you are without contentment and joy, then your life may be dreary, sad and frustrated.

At a primitive level our emotional health is contextualized in our social identity. Humans are, by nature, social animals. Much of our emotional capacity exists for the purposes of navigating social relationships. Our emotional lives are deeply tied to how we interact with our culture, workplaces, families and friends. Therefore, the social fabric we weave into our lives is as essential to our well-being as—possibly more important than—the physical, mental and spiritual domains of our lives. I can be both physically unwell and mentally challenged and still find great joy in my life if I love someone and I am loved. If my social relationships are rich and promote growth, then I am a happier person.

The last four chapters of this section examine the characteristics of a healthy social life and provides an attainable guide for everyone to enrich their connectivity to others. These chapters explore:

- culture and its overarching framework for our social lives—culture is ours to enjoy even when we are most alone

- peers and friends

- deep loves, including husbands, wives, children, parents, Aunt Molly and your dog Sparky

- mentors and teachers

- belonging to community—having a place within one or more tribes

All of us can access these sources of emotional well-being. When our social framework lifts us rather than holds us down, we will invariably experience happiness.

9 Continuous Learning

In the past several chapters, I have described a way to care for our bodies so they can facilitate and be part of our whole, happy self. There is, perhaps, a bit of irony in the fact that the entire section on our physical well-being is approached through an appeal to your mind. As you have read these pages, you were triggered to learn new things, you integrated these thoughts with your own memories of past experiences, you began to incorporate new ideas into your own philosophies, and finally, you planned and committed to new or renewed actions. Your mental domain was at the fore. You thought through a course of options and formulated a path forward of your own making.

In a way that sets you apart from every other species of animals, you took symbols (the text on the pages) and converted them into applicable knowledge, long-term intentions, and concrete ideas and plans. No other animal comes even close to this miraculous achievement. This section of the book is all about not taking this gift for granted. Our intelligence allows a kind of freedom that is unique to humans. Neither driven solely by genetic programming nor clinging and aversive emotions, we are capable of standing back from our reptilian and mammalian cousins and choosing a thoughtful, meaning-filled path forward. Note the word "capable". We are capable of choosing our path, but not all humans exercise this choice. Some of us—all of us at times—are led primarily by our emotional and genetic instincts (reptilian programming for survival).

We want our basic needs met. When we are deprived of these we can become angry, violent or depressed. We want danger and threats to stay away from us. We may fearfully shirk new challenges and constantly scan the environment anxiously, looking for anything that may diminish our security. Emotions and genes may and do master each of us at times. The degree to which we are slaves to our biological needs and untamed emotions is a reflection of our relative freedom. To master our body's needs and our middle-brain's emotions requires the cultivation of our minds. The fact that you are interested in books such as this one indicates that you are already, at minimum, a progressive thinker. Through the facility of deliberate exercise of your mind, you are shaping your life—your body, your emotions and, whether you know it or not, your spiritual being.

As I said in the introduction, the roads go circularly in all directions. Your body, your emotions and your spirit are also shaping your mind. The substantial difference in the nature of the traffic on these multi-directional roads is that your mental domain is the seat of intentionality. When hunger overwhelms you—or excited exuberance causes you to let out a cheer—your mind has little to say. It follows the lead of your other domains. Ideally, however, we would all like to believe that reason and deliberate action would be available to us as often as possible. And when we call upon reasoning and action planning, we would like our mental faculties to serve us well. It's to this fundamental pursuit we now turn, beginning with the topic of continuous learning.

Every parent knows the insatiable demand for explanations that a young child has. My second son was, in particular, a precocious student. Before he could reliably form complex complete sentences, he knew that a one word question usually sufficed. "Why?"

As a three-year-old, he could be counted on to seek an explanation for everything. Why is he required to get dressed? Why is he having toast for breakfast? Why is toast buttered? Why is daddy going to work? Why is the wind blowing? Why don't mommy or daddy know the answer?

I can even remember the sweet boy asking "why?" right up to the moment he fell asleep. We would read him bedtime stories or make them up spontaneously and he would inquire into the actions of our protagonists or antagonists. And each answer given begot another question. His eyes would grow heavy in spite of his ever-present curiosity. And as they became heavier, he would still muster another whispered, "why?" As children do, he would rebel against the urge to sleep until our explanations finally exhausted him. I would tip-toe out of his room, still mumbling some answer, knowing a part of him was still hanging onto the urge to learn. This love of learning—the need to understand our environment—carries forward in all children as they begin their school careers.

In some shape and form we are all curious. Blessed are those who do not let institutionalized learning quash all curiosity. Sadly, for a great many of us, school was not a place for sparkling imaginations and rivers of joyful discovery. "See Tom Run. See Jane Run. See Tom and Jane Run. Jane runs home. Tom runs home. Tom and Jane run home." Ho hum. Grade 1 literature at its finest.

It's a wonder there aren't grumpy protests at every elementary school. Oftentimes, boredom, conformity and regimented rote learning are still the basic means of institutionalized education. This is true in spite of the fabulous gifted men and women who choose to teach our kids. Institutions and bureaucracies stifle originality and spontaneity and, in exchange, they give us a measure of discipline and a degree of consistency. It's a bargain that works well enough for its purposes, but it does take away many people's love of learning.

Our instinct to learn is just that, an instinct. All of us have these large primate brains with an incredible mass of folded tissues with billions of neural cells crowding our cerebral cortexes. Evolution found this development so genetically successful that it continued the growth of the thinking part of the brain such that our heads tend to be at or near the maximum size that can safely escape our mothers' bodies at birth. Unlike most other animals, our brains enter the world with few instructions for survival. We can breathe, suck and, in a limited way, hold on. We are ridiculously dependent on our guardians for at least the first 12 to 14 years of our lives. No other animal devotes the time to child rearing that we humans do. Why is this? Because we evolved to specialize with a complex survival mechanism—thinking.

We learn slowly in order to survive. Many other animals break out from an egg and instantly have all the genetic programming necessary to survive. Even our relatively close cousins such as mice, cats and horses need mere weeks or months to learn to survive on their own. Our uniquely human attribute is to learn extensively to survive in complex social groups with rather minimal physical gifts. We lack multiple stomachs that enable easy grazing. We don't have the speed, agility or claws to attack prey. We are too big to readily hide from tigers and too slow to run away. We learn to survive.

Thus, human infants are born with enormous heads, which—only partially exaggerating—are nearly empty upon arrival. These empty heads never get full. We keep putting more and more knowledge in them and only when we stop learning does the function of the brain decline. Nothing precludes our amazing brains from growing ever more powerful other than reducing our exposure to novel things—items in the environment, academic learning, and our own intrinsic creation of ideas.

Evidence clearly links continuous learning with positive protection from dementia. Scientists know that people who continue to learn through their middle years and into their senior years are much less likely to suffer the kind of cognitive decline characterized by age-related dementia. The implication of this simple discovery is pretty straightforward—use it or lose it. This is no different than the atrophy of our physical bodies. In my past professional life, I never completely stopped being surprised to see the shocking muscular decline when a person's body part was immobilized in a cast. Men and women who spend more than four short weeks immobilized, become so weak that walking or putting a spoon to their mouths is supremely challenging. Why should our brains be any different?

Of course, staving off mental atrophy is by no means the only reason we would want to invest in continuous learning. There is a marvelous joy and satisfaction that comes from learning new things. Naturally, it helps if the thing you are learning about is of interest to you, but paradoxically it's not really necessary. There's a well-documented tendency to grow interested in what we learn about. You've probably seen this in your own life. We've all found ourselves captive in some discussion that, had we seen it coming, we would have dodged it. Have you ever had an expert neighbor tell you about the proper staking methods to support a tomato plant? Or a mechanic explain the inner workings of your car's transmission? Or a dentist explain the reasons for a root canal and how it is done? We've all encountered "an expert" on some subject matter and most of the time we engage just long enough to maintain polite civility. However, you may also often surprise yourself with how you begin to ask engaged questions of the person who is volunteering their expertise. Oftentimes, your curious line of inquiry will lead to zero further interest or action on your part, but you nevertheless went well beyond social graces. You genuinely learned. Why does this happen? It's nothing more than basic human nature. Your brain wants to know things. It likes to be stimulated. It enjoys playing with information.

People who follow their interests have many interests. People who express curiosity grow more curious. People who love to learn—not surprisingly—learn a lot. But what can we do when our love of learning appears deadened? What do we do when we can't identify any interests?

Let's start with an overly simplistic answer. If you want to joyfully engage your brain, become very discerning about all forms of passive, solitary entertainment. The ultimate buzzkill is too much TV and all its spin-offs such as YouTube, Facebook and Netflix.

Research shows that after less than 30 minutes of watching TV, our disposition declines and becomes progressively more depressed with each passing minute. I know exactly how this feels. After a long day, there is nothing more I want than to sit down, put my feet up and watch an enjoyable TV show. I may even have a clear intention of only watching one half-hour episode. Then some three hours later, numb to the world, I can find myself cycling through channels entirely dissatisfied with the content from all 75 programming choices. Finally, late for my usual bedtime, I force myself to power down the hypnotic box, feeling discouraged, disinterested, and wishing I could get back the time wasted.

Not only does TV generally make you feel bad, it pre-empts opportunities to learn something through active, meaningful engagement. Compare watching a re-run of Seinfeld with reading a good book, attending a lecture regarding a passionate interest, joining friends at a wine tasting, researching ideas for a new part-time business, or planning overseas travel. Though the TV program would be entertaining, the other activities will certainly be more engaging and thought-provoking. Of course, there are exceptional programs that I readily enjoy and remain engaged and interested in. This is why I don't suggest you abandon all passive media. Rather, I encourage discerning consumption.

Learning requires a spark to get us started. This is why TV is so addictive. It requires zero effort and holds low quality attention passively for many hours. Real learning, on the other hand, requires some effort. With effort and even a small injection of focused attention, flow can manifest itself. The craftsman who enjoys woodwork can easily spend hours totally immersed in building a beautiful, functional object. But first, he or she has to start.

Creating the activation energy to get started in your pursuit of learning is harder than pressing the button on a remote control. However, once started we know we are in for a much higher quality, self-esteem enhancing experience than any passive entertainment affords us.

So how do you get started? The same way you got started reading this book. You made a choice to pursue personal development rather than passive time killing. Use the same motivation to learn and experience other things.

Try pre-decisions as described earlier. Decide now what you will do later: "After dinner, I will _____." This simple "mind trick" is surprisingly effective. It programs your brain to do what it chose to do at the appointed time.

Another good strategy is to facilitate your action planning by creating less resistance. In other words, make it easier to do what you want to do. Shawn Achor[1], a well-regarded happiness guru, tells a funny story about sleeping in his gym clothes and with his running shoes set beside his bed. When he wakes up, he's dressed for his priority—going to the gym. His shoes are right there. If he doesn't put them on, there is a good chance he'll trip over them. What has he accomplished with these odd behaviors? He removed a few of the obstacles that could stand in the way of doing what's important to him. Before he has even gotten out of bed, he is well on his way to early morning exercise.

There are countless ways you can make your goals easier to pursue. If you want to start your day with a healthy smoothie, put your blender in the center of your countertop with fruit and a protein supplement nestled next to it. If you want to learn to play the guitar, leave your instrument on a stand at the entranceway to your living room. Put your favorite books next to your most comfortable chair under an excellent reading light. Invite a friend to an upcoming lecture and plan to drive together. And perhaps make it harder to do what you don't want to do—take the batteries out of the remote control, cancel your subscription to cable TV, etc.

Be curious. All kinds of people intersect our lives all the time. Find out what interests they have. People are fascinating. Don't be afraid to be weird. Do your thing, whatever it is. Go ahead and be the expert on unicycle world records. Dig for fossils next to your local river. Become the foremost connoisseur of heirloom varieties of green beans. Save the world through the cause that means the most to you, be it global warming, poverty or oppression against women and girls. There are so many things for you to become interested in.

> Be curious. All kinds of people intersect our lives all the time.

Learn and grow. And once you are growing, you will positively glow!

---

1   I recommend Shawn Achor's first book, "The Happiness Advantage".

Points to Ponder:

- What captures your imagination? What passion(s) are you pursuing or wishing to delve deeper into?

- What barriers are getting in the way of doing things you want to do? How could pre-decision help you?

10 Discipline and Ambition

When I was very young, I fell in love with politics. My mom helped a friend with a brief election campaign. I was about 11 years old. My mom's friend had no chance of winning the election. He was only running for office to "show the flag" of his fringe party. Mom didn't even support the party; she was simply being a good friend.

Around the dinner table we talked about some of the main campaign issues. I found them stimulating. As well, I was sure the relevance of the issues directly impacted my own life and the lives of people I cared about. The effort expended by political candidates and their supporters suddenly made sense to me. They wanted to make the world a better place. No one could argue against these motivations. I had caught the bug.

I was infected with politics and the compelling issues of social and economic policy. I began to watch TV news and read the newspaper that I was still delivering in my neighborhood. I read a weekly news magazine. I could speak knowledgeably with adults about the latest polls, the varying policy stances of the competing parties, and I could readily defend my opinions.

Through high school my interest grew. I came to understand the philosophical underpinnings of different political movements. Before I graduated, I knew I needed to travel abroad to see how different countries were shaping their nations through distinct policy choices. And so I travelled.

I studied political science and economics at university after I returned from a year overseas. Throughout my time in university, I was politically active. At one time, I was the president of a university political organization. I participated in debates, organized marches and rallies, and felt deeply that I was part of something important and much bigger than me.

Immediately after obtaining my degree, I found work in a cabinet minister's office as a policy advisor. Less than two years later I served as her chief of staff. We oversaw major, multi-billion dollar operations of government. It was a rush! More than 20 years later, I remain proud of the work I did. Some of those public policies remain in place today.

Now, with many years of separation, I recognize something about my years in politics. When I was hired straight out of university I felt extremely fortunate. And I was. I had never imagined a political career coming to me, except perhaps if I ran for office in my late adult life. But here I was in my early 20s with significant influence over an important area of public policy. I was in regular contact with all the other ministers' staffs. I was a player at the highest levels of provincial political power. How could this be possible?

I had been in training for my role in politics for the prior 13 years. I had studied politics unlike any other kid I knew. My curiosity led me to other parts of the world to examine social policies at work. My academic career was focused on the same subject matter. And I spent at least as many hours doing politics as I did studying politics. My many years of devoted effort led me to my paid political work.

Although I would not have necessarily described myself as disciplined then, I see it clearly now. Year after year, I had a burning desire to make the world a better place. That desire wasn't merely an idle notion that I entertained playfully in my imagination. It was expressed in concrete action—formal study, newspaper addictions, constant discussion with like-minded people, travel, debates and campaigning for my political party.

My current passion—making people happy—has been underway for nearly two decades. I caught onto an early wave of positive psychology and applied it in my own life diligently. It was integrated into my parenting. I found many avenues to practice it in my professional work as a manager of people. I got formal graduate-level training to become a Certified Executive Coach. And my passion ramped up from there, to the point where this pursuit is my full-time occupation. Oftentimes, I can't differentiate between my work and leisure activities.

Before my head gets too big, I need to add that both in my political career and coaching/teaching career, I have had massive set backs. I have made more mistakes than I can count. I've lost coaching clients because I was insensitively honest. I've spoken to audiences where everything I said fell flat. But those failures are along a trajectory of disciplined success. My coaching and teaching gets steadily better because of my failures. The mistakes are part and parcel of success. Knowing this eases many potential regrets.

Failures are along a trajectory of disciplined success.

Discipline is the uncompromising pursuit of a longer term goal, with resilience following failure, and steady effort throughout the journey. Your happy, well-balanced life requires these same three ingredients of discipline: long-term goals, resilience and steady effort. Discipline is both a skill and a mindset. Each can be learned. Skills are methods of undertaking work that can be consistently applied toward achieving defined goals. Mindset is a set of beliefs (convictions) that, when internalized, effortlessly shape behavior.

Simplistically, the skill of discipline could be described as working hard. Yet hard work isn't enough for achieving many goals. It is sustained hard work that makes the difference. Anyone can give 100% effort for a minute, an hour or possibly even a few days. But true accomplishment for any worthy goal requires reasonable effort over much longer time periods. Consider any area of great importance in your own life: physical health, successful relationships, career advancement, or spiritual peace and contentment. What's really valuable to you? No matter your answer, I expect your intention is a long-term goal (unless you chose "winning the lottery"—good luck with that).

Sustaining reasonable effort over long periods can exhaust our willpower. We have many demands on our time and energy. So how do we achieve long-term goals if we constantly run out of the finite supply of willpower? I've had plenty of incomplete projects and several unused gym memberships in my past. Why have some projects come to fruition and others have not?

It boils down to two central ingredients for successful long-term goal attainment. These two things are fundamental to the skill of discipline. The first is the reliance on flow energy—where the energizing activity you undertake is, itself, sufficient to carry effort for extended periods. The second is the constructive use of habits—where behavior is automated to the extent that willpower is unnecessary to start the activity. Let's consider each of these.

Achieving flow is a theme that runs throughout this book. To recap what we learned earlier, flow is a state of focused attention toward the achievement of a specific (generally measurable) goal. In flow, one's skills are being stretched to current abilities, neither bored with something too simple nor overwhelmed by a task too difficult. A person in flow thus grows skill and seeks progressively greater challenge. When in flow, a person loses track of time and the activity is done for its own sake. Imagine trying to undertake a long-term task in which flow is missing. The undertaking becomes drudgery; it's taxing and drains your willpower. So far, I've emphasized personal choice in the pursuit of exercise and other disciplines. This is because flow arises from activity to which we volunteer our hearts and minds. An essential component of this skill of discipline is finding flow. The sister to flow is forming habits.

We are creatures of habit not because we are lazy or insufficiently motivated. Deep in our genetic coding are all kinds of rhythms and patterns that move our biology in necessary steady patterns. We are highly sensitive to the cycles of day and night. We quickly become accustomed to mealtime patterns. Lean into these pre-existing, reliable habits and attach new, self-selected habits. Choose your subject of discipline and do it at the same time and place every day. If your life is regimented around weekends and weekdays, then configure your schedule to include your subject of discipline in a weekend or weekday pattern. Regardless of what you're undertaking, if it's a worthy long-term goal, you must do it regularly over a sustained period so it becomes a habit.

Habits may seem to make more sense for some goals versus others. To write this book I sat at my desk at the same time every weekday. As a bonus, it's a high flow activity for me. But what if discipline is required for a more esoteric goal such as spiritual practice? I set aside time every day for formal spiritual practice; however, informally, I aspire to live my spirituality throughout each day. What if my goal is meeting new people and finding a soul mate? Perhaps more flexibility is required, but habits are still integral to goal achievement. Such a goal might consist of three activities: 1) joining and regularly attending a club, sports team or volunteer organization; 2) daily after dinner management of online dating profiles and responding to interesting inquiries; 3) always eating lunch in your employer's lunch room—not at your desk—and greeting everyone who crosses your path during this time. Habits, habits, habits.

By linking new desired behaviors to existing structures in your day, habits are much easier to form. However, they still require willpower as the habit begins to take hold. I've seen varying research on how long a new behavior must be sustained before it becomes a habit—as little as three weeks to as much as nine weeks. No matter how long it takes, be steadfast. The habit will form and it will stick for as long as you like if your habitual activity is truly generating flow.

We've given considerable attention to the skill of discipline, which is aided by both flow and habits[1]. Now let's consider the mindset of discipline. Unfortunately, people abandoning goals and dreams is a frequent reality. Some of this is the useful pruning of ideas that are unrealistic or, upon reflection, not useful. However, all too frequently, the loss of goals and dreams is tragic and unnecessary. Often, they are simply a breakdown in discipline. The skills of tapping into flow and forming habits are not enough for many of us. An Achilles heel often arises in a failure to overcome setbacks.

I've known a few people who were vanquished when they got close to the finish line. They had a meaningful, worthy goal. They made steady efforts toward obtaining their objective. But then some ONE got in their way. Do you know who it was who put up the barrier? Who derailed a dream from its fulfillment? Almost always it's the person themselves. You, me, we get in our own way.

Carol Dweck is the pre-eminent researcher of our self-imposed barriers. She wrote an excellent book, *Mindset: The New Psychology of Success*, in which she describes learnable skills that can release people from their own mental traps. She differentiates between what she calls fixed and growth mindsets.

A fixed mindset is a belief system that many of us fully or partially embraced during our childhood. We were not conscious of this choice and certainly did not consider the consequences. Yet, during some early period in our lives we came across a challenge that gave rise to us questioning our identity. Dr. Dweck has seen fixed mindsets in children as young as four years old.

Facing some challenge, we knew we could possibly fail. And we believed that failure in the task would reflect on our own fundamental character—who we are. Unwilling to accept ourselves as a "failure" we took a natural path away from the potential label and stood down from the challenge we faced. We walked away from

---

1 Angela Duckworth is perhaps the leading figure in this research. Her book, "Grit: The Power of Passion and Perseverance," is an excellent read.

the goal and the potential for achievement. The threat to our identity was just too great.

Here's a practical example of fixed mindset. A four-year-old is given an easy puzzle to do. She manages the simple task and is invited to do a more difficult puzzle. This very young person has locked into an identity as a successful puzzle maker and she values this identity greatly. So what does she do with the invitation to attempt a more difficult puzzle? She declines because she doesn't want her identity as a success to be threatened. The potential for failure becomes a mental block to continuing her efforts as a puzzle solver.

There may be many reasons why this girl has adopted her fixed mindset—she may receive praise from her parents for her accomplishments and condemnation for her failures. Too much praise for results rather than effort can have unintended consequences. She may also be more risk averse for other reasons. Nevertheless, her fixed mindset leads her to avoid challenges and eschew the effort and persistence required when undertaking a difficult task. Tragically, early adoption of this mindset can hold some people back from pursuing meaningful goals for the rest of their lives.

Now contrast this with someone who has a growth mindset. Imagine a different little girl. She completes the same easy puzzle and takes pride in her effort. She may recognize that although, at first, she put some pieces into the puzzle incorrectly, she was able to correct her errors and assemble the complete puzzle. When invited to do a more difficult puzzle, she relishes the opportunity to grow her skills. Moreover, when she finds the pieces not easily going into their correct places, she perseveres knowing that errors and multiple tries are part of her process. When she successfully completes the puzzle, her identity as someone who learns through persistent practice is reinforced. She sees errors—failure—as a natural part of learning.

Those with a growth mindset see challenges as opportunities.

This example of puzzle building may seem rather trivial, but in the whole of life the difference between a fixed and growth mindset can make all the difference with respect to goal achievement. People with a fixed mindset generally don't take on difficult challenges; whereas those with a growth mindset see challenges as opportunities. Fixed mindset people believe they have a certain limited amount of talent and intelligence. By contrast, growth mindset people see talent and intelligence as outcomes flowing from effort. They are confident in their ability to make things happen in their own lives. With effort and persistence, growth mindset people manufacture their future. Fixed mindset people see little value in sustained effort, so they give up when larger challenges present themselves. The world is generally a threatening place for fixed mindsets, so they tend to live small and settle for less.

Truly fantastic research demonstrates that people with fixed mindsets can learn to have growth mindsets. And people who unconsciously were fortunate to grow up with a growth mindset, can further understand their own power to overcome challenge. Learning a growth mindset is not all that profound. Several key concepts are all that are necessary to understand the growth mindset:

- Effort counts—the more you put in, the more you get out.
- Failure is part of growth. Accept it—again and again—by getting back on the track to your goals.
- Everyone, including you, can grow and change.
- Passion and persistence always pays off; therefore, your true potential is unknowable.

Please read these four statements again. Learn them. Write them down and post them on your fridge. Say them out loud twice every day. Soon you will have not just learned these concepts, but you will begin to believe them. Your daily life will begin to express your beliefs. You will see that deliberate practice can accomplish so very much. Your goals will come toward you as you take on challenges knowing that you can learn your way through a process of accomplishment. Your identity will become that of a "do-er". You will not only get stuff done, but you will also be your own best friend because the "do-er" in you will get your agenda accomplished.

Fixed mindsets limit one's vision and prop up a person's ego by defending some current level of success. You are reading this book because you know you are not limited by your current circumstances. You can change your circumstances and in doing so, you will change. You are capable of growing your own creativity, intelligence and talent in any field of your choosing. There is no magical thinking that promises to turn you into a Warren Buffet, Katy Perry or Lebron James, but you can most definitely be a bigger, more powerful, more radiant you. Your potential is unknowable. Go test it for yourself!

To recap, discipline is a basic building block in your mental domain. It consists of finding flow in your activities, building habits and adopting a growth mindset. Discipline is a mental muscle. If you cultivate discipline, you grow the muscle. Just like a muscle, however, it also fatigues. We all need rest, relaxation and wholeness—balance in our physical, mental and spiritual domains. Be patient with yourself if you find discipline difficult. Nevertheless, you will need to exercise discipline regularly—flow, habits and a growth mindset.

Now that we know all about discipline, what do we do with it?

Ambition

Goals are like fuel for the soul. Yes, they need to be well supported by discipline, but first, good goal setting is essential.

People who accomplish a lot are often list makers. They get stuff done. However, this book is not about things you can cross off today's to-do list. This book is about longer-term, whole life goals. It's about being a complete, integrated person—a person full of meaning and purpose across all domains: body, mind and spirit. It's about the felt experience of frequent positive emotions. It's about you feeling a deep satisfaction about who you are (your character) and what you do (your gifts to the world). In order to set goals in this context, you need to take stock of your most deeply held values.

Values are what we believe are the most important qualities of our lives. They are the characteristics we most want to manifest in our work, relationships and lifestyle. Values that are properly understood ground us in the beliefs and activities that support what gives us mental energy. When I am truly excited and highly motivated to do some specific thing, there is always a critical, personal value underlying the project.

If you are somewhat ambivalent about which goals are most important to you, you will benefit from doing some work to identify your core values.

Knowing our values is key to a contented life. By seeing life as a set of options from which to choose, we are made free. However, when we don't know what we value most, we may find ourselves chasing after goals that don't satisfy us. There are many values and a person may identify with nearly all of them—wealth, honesty, control, service, security, empathy, usefulness, discretion…and on and on. All these words, and hundreds more, describe characteristics that can appeal to nearly everyone. However, each of us has a short list—10 or fewer—of our truly most important personal values. When we know these values, we know where our mental energy can be most readily engaged.

Real liberty comes when we choose from life's copious options to do what is aligned with our deepest values. If you know your values and how you rank them, decision-making is infinitely easier. I've coached many middle-aged people who found themselves in a busy conquest of other people's goals—parents, school teachers, spouses, even popular culture. Wrong careers, misplaced financial priorities, empty leisure—people wake up to all manner of activities to find that they are alienated from their own lives. Fortunately, when these same clients learn about and take active ownership of their values, they energize their lives. Options worthy of their effort become apparent. People begin to live with greater integrity and in alignment with ethical behaviors when they are consciously living their deepest values.

Living your values is very much a mental discipline—it's about a reasoned choice from a broad set of possible values. Once you know your most important values, you will have new insights into life's priorities, including career, health, family and other goals.

Note that you may be surprised by some of the values you choose as your most important and you may realize that some things you used to hold essential no longer matter to you. This is common and natural. As you grow, gain life experience, and accomplish the tasks of youth and young adulthood, there is almost always a shift in your core values. For the most part, you will shift gradually and not many times throughout your life. But because values do shift, reflecting deeply on your values may be useful to you every few years, particularly when you question the direction and meaning of your life.

On my website, www.HappinessExperts.ca, the Resources tab has several excellent exercises. Take the time to try one or more of them. You will then have a short list of your most deeply held values and you can consider their connection to your ambitions.

If you know your values, your ambitions become clearer. If you have a goal that isn't congruent with your values, it's time to pause. Are you pursuing someone else's goal that has been foisted onto you? Consider the goal carefully. If it really is your goal, link it to your deeply held values. If it does not connect with an identified value, perhaps spend some more time with the exercises on my website. Your values and your long-term goals must connect; otherwise you will waste your precious muscle of discipline on a pursuit that will not satisfy you. By contrast, when your long-term goals are born out of your most important values, you turbo-charge your discipline.

It's basic math: ambition (rooted in values) + discipline (flow, habits and a growth mindset) = your dreams coming true.

Points to Ponder:

- What areas of your life are presently well disciplined? Can you celebrate this accomplishment in a meaningful way?

- What habits do you want to form to help you achieve a long term goal?

- What's your mindset? How will you address the areas of life where you have accepted a fixed mindset belief about yourself?

- What ambition stirs a fire inside you? What can you do this week to fuel this desire, even in some small way?

11 Creativity and Curiosity

A couple years ago, my then-16-year-old son, David, engaged in an hours-long experiment with a tiny computer, a Raspberry Pi. It's about the size of a man's wallet and did all the things a normal computer does: word processing, games, web searches, etc. It even played high definition video. It had limitations due to its small memory but I'm surprised how robust it was.

David was quite interesting to observe as he played with this tiny computer rather than his high-end gaming computer. He gave me a brief explanation, which I didn't really understand, but I could see a keyboard was hooked up to the Raspberry Pi, which was hooked up to our big screen TV. On the TV was a black screen with short lines of white code on the left margin scrolling down the entire height of the screen.

I made dinner and the kids helped; however, David was eager to get back to his task. Different wires/connectors were sought and found and code continued to be input. At one point, the Raspberry Pi was disconnected from the TV display and hooked up to his gaming computer. At another point, he was controlling the input to the Raspberry Pi from his iPad. Periodically, he would search the internet to learn how to do something. Occasionally, David's little brother, Paul, would ask a question and suggest applications that "they" should do with the Raspberry Pi.

A few minutes after 10 p.m., I wished David a good night and encouraged him not to stay up too late. He was on his hands and knees typing on the keyboard into the Raspberry Pi. I have no idea what time it was when he finally stopped.

He was not doing this thing, whatever it was, for school. I am certain he had no vision of creating a use for the Raspberry Pi that would make him money. The simple truth is he was playing. But, oh my! What a sight it was. His intensity, excitement and ambition were palpable. David busily moved his keyboard around to different devices, and 25-foot cables snaked around the room as he connected and disconnected the iPad, computer tower and the big screen TV to the Raspberry Pi. Our home was temporarily converted to a computer programming hub. We were immersed in a technology-coated burst of creativity. It was clearly a flow activity for my son, and yet it was more than that. He was inventing new uses—new to him, at least—for his device. He was completely absorbed in the joy of unleashed creativity.

I'm thrilled just thinking about it. As with other aspects of parenting, I got to share in the emotional rewards gained from the labour of my son's applied skills.

This is too often a rare circumstance in most homes, including mine. Schools still generally emphasize rote learning. Individual curiosity is sacrificed for conformist, regimented instruction. Children's sports are overseen by rule-bound adults. Playtime is linear with spoon-fed TV programs or video games with prescribed storylines and campaigns. For goodness sake, our kids even receive their Lego kits with prescribed instructions for assembling a particular object.

Our adult lives are generally no better. Like robots, we march off to work and, more than anything else, struggle to perform as expected. We cookie cutter produce whatever is required of us—reports from templates, customer service with scripted talking points, factory production with quotas measured by the second, and homes built row by row with minimal individualization. It can feel like there's a blueprint for everyone and every task. Curiously, even in environments where new ideas and innovation are necessary, mavericks are eliminated or assimilated. It's special, indeed, to find truly creative outlets in paid employment. Many adults then return home and, like their kids, generally consume passive pre-scripted forms of entertainment: TV, internet and video games.

Nature is 100% committed to creativity.

Fortunately, nature persists within us. And nature is 100% committed to creativity. We all find blissful moments of curiosity and creativity. Blessed be the cook who sees recipes as mere inspirational sources to which he can add novel ingredients and create something unique. Blessed be the home decorator who is not trying to replicate a magazine picture, but finds colors and shapes and styles that please her own senses. Blessed be the gardener who designs and creates his own Eden. Blessed be the musician who savors her own chord combinations. Blessed be the family that deliberately engages in free discussion about arts, culture and politics. Blessed be the writer, woodworker, painter, seamstress, and all craftsman and artists who make their own unique mark. They will have joy and inspired intellects. They will boost self-esteem and reduce stress. They will feel free, living with risk and reward, independent of the cultural pressure to conform. They will tell their own story— quiet or loud, sad or proud. They will be in touch with nature's most powerful expression: abundant, unceasing creativity.

Have you ever noticed how creative people—all of us, actually—not only make original objects, but they also see problems from new perspectives? The lesson learned continuously from creative expression is that there are novel ideas, novel ways of knowing. People who exercise their creativity find life's challenges—our every day problems—easier to manage. Their enhanced thinking styles, exercised and developed through creative undertakings, spontaneously contribute to them seeing problems from a different perspective. People who exercise creativity find ways over or around obstacles, while others give up because they can't see a way through a problem.

Creativity has the many benefits alluded to above, but that's not all. Creativity generates flow; it is its own reward. Exercising creativity is fun and absorbing. It grows skills.

So how does a person exercise their inherent creativity?

Be curious! Curiosity is the foundational character from which new ideas arise. Curiosity in and about life will grow creativity. Try it! Look, listen, feel and think longer, and with more intensity than you ordinarily do and you will be nurturing your own creativity. All the world is an inspiration. If that advice is too general, then pick a specific existing interest and start learning.

Experiential learning is best. If you can "do" something to learn rather than read a book or watch a video, the learning will be more potent. You could read all about gardening, but until you have put a spade in the ground, your curiosity and creativity are minimized. A woodworker may watch dozens of YouTube tutorials, but must actually shape wood to be deeply learning. Even subjects that are naturally suited to bookish learning—philosophy, for example—is made more real and delves more deeply when we talk and write about ideas.

Whenever we allow our curiosity to grow our expertise, we are becoming equipped to be more creatively expressive. With little knowledge and experience, I have little to work with; my voice is muted. With much knowledge and experience, my output is capable of more nuanced, and often original, content. Creative people are adaptive. They adjust to new situations by bringing novel thinking, taking risks, and leaving their agendas of what "should" be to the side while what "is" emerges.

Follow your curiosity. Play with it. Take a new route home from work. Read a newspaper you don't usually pick up. Take a class on a subject you know nothing about. And if you already have a deep passion, ask yourself what it would take to deepen your knowledge and experience to a whole new level. And then do it!

Points to Ponder:

- What routine are you willing to shake up? What will you do differently? When, specifically, will you start?

- What activity from your past stirred your creative juices and gave you a lot of pleasure? How could you get some of that back into your life?

12 Critical Thinking

Critical thinking is a mental skill that everyone has to a lesser or greater extent. It's the ability to investigate and then employ reason to arrive at sound conclusions. Cultivating this skill is immensely practical for all kinds of problem solving. To confidently gather evidence, evaluate what you've learned and make a sound decision gives you much peace of mind. How do you choose a cell phone service, a car, or a vacation destination? How do you create a financial plan or evaluate a teacher? All these considerations are best undertaken with a clear dose of rational, critical thinking.

Given this book's emphasis on whole-person balance, you may not be surprised to learn that I also recognize and endorse the intuitive, emotional component that goes into making decisions of importance. We all need to listen to our gut and explore what's driving our enthusiasm or dread. However, I fret a bit when I see someone make a decision based solely on gut feelings. Too often, people's emotions lead them astray. This has caused great pain even in my own life. When feelings are strong enough, I can rationalize almost anything. The gift of critical thinking is that it provides space to stand back from action long enough to give our mental faculties a chance to serve us. The bigger the decision, the more thoroughly one ought to deeply investigate options and their potential consequences.

The interplay between emotional drives and reasoning is most confused when it comes to our own lives. Our ability to understand our own circumstances and choose a course forward is often clouded by numerous emotions and rationalizations that fly under the radar of our conscious awareness. I commonly meet with clients who are stuck in some predicament they don't like—an unsatisfying job, a poor relationship, unhealthy habits related to food and exercise and so on. By the time they meet with me, they generally have considered their "problem" for protracted periods, sometimes even years. It's easy to empathize because challenges such as changing jobs, ending relationships and breaking old habits is not easy, nor, perhaps, should it be. These clients get stuck in a narrow component of critical thinking: the investigation or evidence-gathering phase.

Investigating options for life's big questions can be endless. Our lifestyle, which consists of our work, our spiritual practices, our relationships with others, and our relationships with our bodies is of fundamental importance to each of us. Without criticism, these characteristics of our identity make up our essential egos. When we are contemplating change to core concepts of our ego, many of us get stuck investigating options or gathering evidence for the need to change. This stuck-ness grows painful because we want either a new action or a firm decision to be content with what is. And when stuck-ness is deeply engrained, it can lead to anxiety, depression and plummeting self-esteem. We tell ourselves, at least at some level of awareness, that we are not in control of our lives. Being out of control for a moment on a carnival ride can be fun. Being out of control over our lifestyle and our identity for any prolonged period is deeply discouraging.

What drives stuck-ness?

Fear.

Fear is at the root of all protracted investigatory (evidence gathering) stages of critical thinking. Fear is a healthy, biologically well-evolved experience for us to have. Its evolutionary purpose was designed to serve us in the moment as a break or accelerator on action during a specific point in time. Fear of the sabre-tooth tiger served our ancestors well; it's good not to be eaten. Fear of social rejection makes sense; banishment from ancient tribes would usually result in premature death. Fear is okay, even though we don't like how it feels. It should, and often does, preclude us from taking impulsive actions affecting our lifestyle and identity.

Fear should stop me from telling off my boss when I become frustrated. Fear serves me well when I refrain from abandoning a love relationship when I get frustrated. Fear in these contexts is appropriate and helpful. It's the more primitive part of our brain assisting us in basic survival. However, as we all know, chronic fear is debilitating. When fear, and its companion emotions of anxiety and shame, stick around for lengthy periods, then we are stuck in an unhealthy pattern.

My clients who are stuck often want to discuss problem-solving solely from a dispassionate, rational point of view. They know they're stuck. They believe, or hope, that some assistance with their decision-making process will provide a rational solution to their problem. But, to address their stuck-ness, they must first get in touch with the emotional block before they can solve the "mechanical" problem of what careers, relationships and lifestyles to pursue. For some clients this is easy. They may even be fully aware of the fear and anxiety or shame that has them stuck. For others, it takes probing to help them see the source of their stuck-ness. And some clients walk away from the coaching process, unable to witness their own vulnerability.

Interestingly, the solution to being stuck in this early part of the critical thinking process—investigating/evidence gathering—is resolved by applying critical thinking processes. If we can recognize that we are stuck, then we need to examine the underlying emotion through the lens of critical thinking.

Before we examine a model for critical thinking, it's necessary to consider emotional awareness as a step in and of itself. If you're stuck in some part of your life and you know this to be true because it has caused you angst for a significant period, can you identify the emotion? Is it fear? Fear is connected to the potential for loss. Will something you greatly value be threatened if you take action? Is it anxiety? Anxiety is rooted in uncertainty about the future and a natural desire for security. Is it shame? Shame has its roots in a belief that one's behavior falls outside of one's own, or society's, ethical boundaries.

Any one of these feelings and sometimes a combination of them are the emotional block that leads to a person feeling stuck. A deep consideration of the emotion(s) is always warranted. Rather than pushing away fear, anxiety or shame, try to embrace it. Own it. After all, it's your fear. It exists in you. You produced it and, ultimately, only you can deal with it. Moreover, it's normal. We all have fear. Millions of other humans most likely have fear very similar to your own. Like you, these are other good people trying to make their way in the world with happiness and kind intentions. Your fear won't go away by ignoring it. Fear will rule subversively if it isn't shown the light of day.

When you see your fear, greet it warmly.

I once heard Buddhist monk Thich Naht Hanh talking about negative emotions in a delightful way.

He said, when you see your fear, greet it warmly. With kindness, like meeting an old friend, invite your fear in for a cup of tea. Come to your fear and say to it, "Hello, old friend. I see you. Will you come and have tea with me? Please sit down. I want to understand you. Please spend some time with me". I love this perspective. Our fear is with us anyway. Why not get to know it? "Where did you come from, old friend? What do you see and know?"

I've seen this approach work miracles for clients and in my own life. Our negative emotions block our desired behaviors and goals only when we fail to address them. For most people, simply accepting and understanding their emotions is sufficient to drain their power. They may not recede completely, but they are put back into perspective. Fear is given its proper weight, along with all the other considerations in your life planning. Instead of being a hidden trump card that keeps us stuck, fear is just a part of life like lower pay at a new job, excitement at the prospect of committing to a new relationship, or a concrete plan for exercise.

Fear and other emotions that keep us stuck can be considered in the following critical thinking model. In multi-faceted challenges the model needs to be used repetitively. When we are stuck, first apply the model to the emotional block and once it's understood, the model can be applied to your real interest in considering identity and lifestyle.

Critical thinking model

1. Challenge identification

Often, defining a challenge or problem (like native emotions) is the biggest component in solving a puzzle. Write your problem down. What is the top-of-mind, natural expression of what your gut says about your predicament? Now that you've written your problem down, consider it from another perspective. Ask how a neutral, third party observer would define the challenge. Write that down too. Now ask how your inner child would see the problem. The little girl or boy who wants to feel safe and loved—how does she or he see the problem? Write it down. You can keep choosing perspectives to help get clarity on the nature, size and fulsome context of the challenge. What is the challenge from the perspective of a financial advisor? Marriage counsellor? Good friend? Naturopathic clinician? Spiritual guide? Lawyer? Try whatever works and adds value. In my experience, the neutral third party and the inner child often have good insights. Once you have a variety of perspectives, consolidate your definition of the challenge to one rounded statement that incorporates multiple perspectives.

2. Gather your evidence

This step may be easy or hard depending on the challenge that's been defined in step one. Nevertheless, it is an essential step. What can be seen, heard and learned to prove that the challenge is as you defined it? When you identify the cause of the problem, don't settle for superficial first answers. There are nearly always causes for the causes. Look deeply at your evidence. Dig at least one or two layers down.

3. Identify your options

Along with the status quo, what else is there? Usually, there are subtle variations to the status quo. Don't overlook these. Do you need a massive behavior change, or might one or two minor changes make a big difference? Think outside the box. An approach like the following often opens ideas: If you had a magic wand, and with one stroke of the wand you could completely eliminate your problem, what would be different? If that perfect solution is a massive 10 on a scale of 1 to 10, where are you now on that scale? What would move you just one number closer to 10? Try it. Create several options.

4. Weigh your options

What rational, evidence-based facts point to the best resolution? Remember to keep your emotions in context. Only once you have analyzed them can you do this step with integrity. Are there unstated assumptions that are causing you to give more weight to some options over others? What are these assumptions?

5. Commit to a decision

Are you going to take the action that you judge to be best? You won't know if your decision is vague. If you can't put your answer into the SMART matrix you haven't yet reached a meaningful decision. Is your decision:

S – Specific: Clearly identifiable and distinct

M – Measurable: How will you know if you are truly taking the desired actions? If there are no short-term measures to indicate whether you are on track, your decision is not yet specific. Measures need to be, at minimum, monthly. Daily is better.

A – Attainable: Is your decision based on fantasy or can you truly make it happen with hard work and perseverance?

R – Relevant: Does your solution genuinely address your original challenge?

T – Time-bound: Given the nature of some life goals, there's nothing inherently wrong with having long time horizons for some goals. However, goals as a motivation for action are virtually useless if time horizons can't be broken down into near-term increments. Where do you need to be in a month? Six months? A year? What action happens today?

An example of the model at work:

John is considering a career change. He feels stuck, but has worked through and accepts the fear that is preventing any action from occurring. He vaguely knows he's not getting much satisfaction from his job and oftentimes he's discouraged as he prepares to go to the office.

1. Challenge Identification:

John's first answer: I don't like my job.

John's 3rd Party Advisor: Looking from the outside, the job looks ok. There's decent pay and pretty reasonable working conditions including the high likelihood of job security for the foreseeable future.

John's inner child: I'm bored. I want more fun. I can't get excited about any of the projects assigned to me.

John's consolidated definition of the challenge: Although there are some good material benefits to my job, I am lacking stimulation. I long for something that truly captures my interests and stretches my skills.

2. Gather Evidence:

First layer of evidence: I've been in the same position for five years. I know the job inside and out. My boss is good to me, and the pay and benefits are not the problem. I used to enjoy the work when I first started. It was interesting and I had a sense that the company was going places. There are no major changes expected and I am stagnating.

Second layer of evidence: I've been in the same job for five years because there is no natural promotional opportunity and, even if my boss was leaving, I may not have the qualifications to advance. In this region of the country, the pay and benefits are more than fair. Some internet research shows I would likely take a cut in pay if I sought employment somewhere else. My wife, however, has a great job she loves. We could afford to live with a modestly lower household income if we wanted to. I liked the job for the first couple of years because I was constantly learning new things. I was interested in developing the quality initiative because I became immersed in every aspect of our production chain. Every day now seems to be just going through the motions. I'm bored because I have ceased growing.

3. Option Identification:

Status quo: Keep doing what I'm doing. Seek greater flow from non-work activities.

Get a diploma: Stay at work, but get my diploma at night school so I will qualify for my boss's job. The company may pay for my education and this may give me the flow opportunity I'm looking for. I love it when I'm learning new things.

Change careers: I always wanted to work with my hands. I should pursue a construction job. I have a lot of skills and, if I grow my expertise, I could start my own company.

4. Weigh Options:

Status quo: My pay and benefits are enticing and I'm scared of leaving, but the truth is I don't want to live a life wishing, wondering "if only I had chosen a different path". I deserve to be happier at work, particularly given how much time I devote to it. I could try to make life better outside of work in order to offset my dissatisfaction on the job, but I already have a full and enjoyable life outside work. My current job needs to change.

Get a diploma: There are no guarantees that I would get my boss's job, nor do I know if and when he will leave his position. I do like the idea of getting my diploma all the same. If I get it, my job options and pay potential will be greater whether I stay with my current employer or if I find a new company to work for.

Change careers: This idea gets me excited and it could really work out well. I'm still young enough and healthy enough to start a new, physical line of work. I have several friends in the construction industry who could connect me with potential employers. My pay would go down at first, but our household income would still be more than adequate.

5. Decision Commitment:

After investigating my employer's willingness to pay a portion of my tuition costs, I have decided to enroll in the diploma program.

Apply the SMART matrix:

Specific: I will get my diploma.

Measurable: I can take one online course over the summer. I will get signed up and buy the books this week. Next fall, I will begin night courses.

Attainable: This will be a pile of work, but I can totally do this. My wife is supporting my choice and her steadfastness will be a resource I can draw from. I will do it!

Relevant: My employer is good to me. I just need more challenge. Schooling will do that and it will definitely open up more doors for me.

Time-bound: By the end of this month I will be enrolled in the online course and the fall online classes. By this time next year I will have five courses complete. In less than two years I will complete the diploma program. Hooray!

This short example left out a lot of detail, but it showed John's process of moving from stuck-ness to an energized place of moving forward. He exercised a valuable set of critical thinking skills to reach a definitive, meaningful solution to his challenge. And he addressed his fears head-on in his deliberations. His emotions did not hijack his efforts; rather, they were part of his rational considerations and were given the weight they deserved.

John's use of critical thinking created opportunity. Using his mental domain and specifically facing his emotions within a critical thinking process gave him energy and motivation. He'll require discipline and courage as he moves forward. Yet, we can be confident that our hypothetical John is expanding his being. He's growing. He's seeking greater flow.

You and I will do the same!

Critical thinking is a skill that can be practiced and improved. Its regular use keeps you mentally sharp. With consistent application you will find decision making easier and more effective. You will be confident as you make substantial purchases and important life decisions. Moreover, if you routinely apply critical thinking to your emotions, you'll feel a tremendous freedom from fear ruling your behaviors. Fear will be given its proper place as an input and nothing more.

I have an excellent personal analysis tool that I often use with clients. The tool is called Personal Groundwork for Coaching and it provides a framework to consider the balance and sources of frustration and joy in your life. It allows you to understand the state of your relationships, health, money, career and more. Many of my clients have used this tool as an effective starting point for launching their next stage of personal growth. If you are curious about it, please email me at Paul@HappinessExperts.ca. Even if you know with certainty what part of your life you want to work on, this analysis tool can give you power as you learn with gratitude what areas of your whole person are on track. Often, you will find one or two small, easy-to-overcome challenges that, when you tackle them, you have extra capacity to undertake the work for which you have a passion.

Points to Ponder:

- What are you afraid of? Think deeply. In what area of your life do you feel unsatisfied? What's holding you back?
- Apply the critical thinking model to the place of stuck-ness in your life.

13 Love

Reptiles need very little emotional support. From an evolutionary perspective, they benefit from simple feelings like pain, fear and contentedness. This helps them avoid dangers, seek sustenance and know when to rest. Along with their short memories, their blunt emotional life must make life relatively easy to manage. Reptiles are, therefore, excused from reading this chapter.

Fortunately for humans, our mammalian brains evolved a capacity for richer feelings; just watch a cat purr or a dog wag its tail. Evolution then took another giant leap with primate brains. Our emotional experience is at an entirely different level from most of our mammalian cousins. Primate brains have the feelings of attachment and belonging as central components of our existence. Descendants of apes read on!

In primates, emotions are most often contextualized within relationships, with a few exceptions. Fear, pain, hunger and a few other basic survival guides don't require relationships. As well, we enjoy experiences that are solitary, but elicit feelings of satisfaction and awe. Besides those important exceptions, our vast and emotionally complicated experiences are generally situated in the presence of social contexts. Is there another person—or some animal or thing to which we have grown attached—present when we experience the following emotions?

- Disappointment

- Contempt

- Anger

- Embarrassment

- Tenderness

- Pride

- Compassion

- Amusement

Of course, there is a host of other emotions that we feel within relationships, including many nuances of happiness and sadness.

This part of the book focuses on the social fabric that makes up so much of our emotional lives. Perhaps no research findings regarding happiness and well-being is more clear than the significance of good relationships. Where they are present, people thrive. Where there is an absence of healthy and warm relationships, life is difficult.

One does not have to look far to understand why this is so. Secure, warm attachments to other humans was absolutely essential to the survival of our ancestors. To be alone was often a death sentence. Nearly defenseless as a singular person on the African Savannah, we would be easy prey for a pack of lions or hyenas. Moreover, evolution's drive to express our genes in future generations requires social engagement. Human babies are slow to reach maturity. There is enormous labor associated with their care; the simple burden of carrying them goes on for years. Successful child rearing benefits from committed partners remaining together for at least several years. Without strong bonds between parents, and from parents to children, few children would thrive.

As a result of the labour of raising kids and the significant security advantages in groups, humans have evolved to have an imperative for social bonding. Like pack wolves or dolphins or chimpanzees, humans have a need that goes beyond pair bonding. We thrive in communities of many members, from tribes with several dozen people to cities with millions.

Nature found that amongst mammals, the way to create successful groups was to instil powerful emotional incentives to belong. No emotion is more painful than loneliness. To be cast out from the warmth and support of a community feels as crippling as any injury. By contrast, to be respected, cared for, and securely attached to a loving community is one of life's greatest pleasures. Our emotions generally sanction us—make us feel bad—when we behave contrary to the interests of our tribe. And when warmly embraced by someone with whom we share deep bonds of love, we feel exquisitely good.

> To be respected, cared for, and securely attached to a loving community is one of life's greatest pleasures.

There's no doubt that throughout all of history up to the period of the Industrial Revolution, our social groups were mostly made up of family—people who shared a close genetic heritage and a cohesive commitment to the survival of all its members. Family, amongst successful tribes, included cousins, aunts, uncles, grandparents, brothers and sisters.

Industrial activity led to an ease of travel that made separation over long distances affordable and easy. Instead of entire tribes searching for more hospitable environments, for the last 200 to 300 years individuals have been able to go seek their fortune alone. The extended family in most western cultures remains biologically connected, but not remotely similar to the close daily bonds of yesteryear. This undoubtedly causes existential yearning for great swaths of humanity. Still, most of us today try to preserve and/or create a reflection of tribal family bonds.

We keep in touch with the people with whom we shared a home as children. We generally love and stay emotionally close to our parents and siblings. Yet, for most people the bonds of daily communion we knew as children are substantially diminished, with families fracturing as people move away to different cities and countries. At best, we remain within a few blocks of some members of our immediate family. This leaves many of us struggling to reconcile our fractured family ties.

One thing is certain: the potential for loneliness has never been greater. We all share a deep need—our biological heritage—to create a meaningful, loving bond with one or more people. For many people, we manage this extraordinary feat in a marriage and with the addition of children. Of course, committed long-term friendships can fill much of this need, and in some respects can do so with fewer of the downsides found in navigating family life.

Ed Diener is one of the leading researchers on happiness within relationships. His many studies show resolutely that happy people are more extroverted and more likely to be in strong, supportive relationships. In addition, the reward of strong, supportive relationships is greater happiness. A magnetic, reinforcing pattern: happiness leads to friends and good friends lead to happiness.

To me, these research findings point to an obvious conclusion. Our efforts to be connected in committed, warm relationships are well-founded. Relationships characterized by love are the most valuable to our well-being.

Love is most often found in our closest family relationships—spouses, children, parents, and often other extended family. Characteristics of the best kinds of family relationships include the following:

- Acceptance — Even of our weaknesses.

- Support — Cheerleaders for our triumphs and a shoulder to cry on in our tragedies.

- Pride — Our accomplishments give satisfaction to our loved ones.

- Care — Practical meeting of needs in sickness and in health.

- Fun — Play and humor are encouraged.

- Appreciation — Acknowledgement of a valuable bond with another.

When relationships with family have these characteristics, we feel safe in an environment that can be described by the word "love". These same characteristics are found in close friendships. Love is not solely the domain of family.

Take stock of your own social circumstances. Do you have one or more relationships that have all these characteristics—acceptance, support, caring, pride, fun and appreciation? If your answer is a confident "yes", then congratulations. You are indeed a lucky person blessed with a special gift. Your life is undoubtedly better for having love in it. If your answer was qualified in some way—maybe most of the characteristics of love are present, but imperfectly so—you still have much to be grateful for. If your answer was "no", this is a serious wake up call. But take heart; relationships are build-able. No matter how you answered the question, you can benefit from considering your investment in loving relationships.

Most of us know the pain of broken relationships. When people should not be together—where abuse or clear incompatibility are present—ending a relationship is wise. But where good will and trust can be forged in secure relationships, the payoffs are huge. So what does it take to have successful relationships?

While no perfect recipe exists, a few things are clear. When we consciously invest in the quality and character of our relationships, there are returns. Words and actions are our basic tools.

Speak a high positivity ratio

One researcher stands above all others when it comes to intimate relationships. I have attended an excellent conference and read several books by noted researcher Dr. John Gottman. His persuasive findings are based on years of observing couples interact. Dr. Gottman has found that thriving, happy couples have five positive interactions for every one negative interaction. Ratios of positive to negative interactions that are less than three to one are deadly to long-term partnerships. This finding is not so shocking. In the practical activity of normal family life, there are many entirely neutral interactions. We share household duties, pass food at the table, watch TV, etc. Our discussions may be instrumental to getting things done: "Please pass the salt", "Did you buy milk?", etc. These conversations may neither generate positivity nor negativity. When an interaction is negative, it stands out in our experience. We have a twinge (or worse) of negative emotion: anger, disappointment, shame or hurt. We do not recover readily from powerfully negative interactions. If our spouse yells at us or uses derogatory language, it carries major weight. This is the reason relationships need the high positive to negative ratio of five to one; it takes a lot of positive interactions to counteract a few negative interactions. Achieving these high ratios makes for a happy relationship.

Manufacturing this high ratio is something we can work towards. Obviously, contributing lots of positive comments is important, but it's also key to minimize negativity from our speech. We must avoid harsh judgment and criticism whenever possible. (As noted before, abuse is not to be tolerated and calls for action separate from the context of this discussion). We are all guilty of many small transgressions—an item of laundry left out, toothpaste on the bathroom counter, being a bit late without calling, forgetting to buy milk… Can we overlook the weaknesses and foibles of the people we love? If not these people, then to whom can we be gracious? Oddly, it is often easier—more socially expected—to not comment on errors made by mere acquaintances. At the same time, we sometimes feel the need to point out the "errors" of loved ones.

What a tremendous gift it is to give your loved ones real acceptance. Be gracious. Cut them some slack. Overlook minor errors and small transgressions. What would this do for the people you love? Your company would be a time and place of warmth, trust and safety. This is advice I find remarkably difficult to live by. Yet, when I can mindfully lay off my family members' faults for even a couple days, I notice a positive change in the environment. If an occasional mistake becomes a regular problem, then you may need to address it. All relationships occasionally require honest communication to sort out points of tension. Choose carefully when and if this is really necessary. How impressive and generous would it be if you could raise the mistake outside of the immediate context of the problem. Instead of barking as you see the sock fall to the floor, wait 20 minutes or more until a moment of relative tranquility. Then, with calmness and love, state your need from the perspective of your experience. The "error" is not about your "slob" of a spouse; rather, it is about your own felt experience. "Honey, when I see your socks on the floor, I feel discouraged. I like the house to be clean and I would be grateful if you could pick up after yourself." Then leave it alone. If your spouse's worst transgressions are relatively minor, why jeopardize the positivity ratio with unnecessary criticism and judgment. Genuinely let it go.

Avoiding negative speech as much as possible will substantially add to the quality of most relationships. Conversely, adding to the positive side of the equation may also be easier than you think. Consider how much neutral activity occurs that neither positively nor negatively affects your relationship. There is ample opportunity in the mundane to appreciate the blessings of people in your life.

I am careful about how I criticize my two sons. When I am conscious of how I want our interactions to be—that is, overwhelmingly positive—I see so much opportunity to increase the kindness between us. Of course, I am fortunate in that my boys are generally quite amicable. Still, I want them to know that I see that. I do a lot of cooking and I usually enlist the help of one or both of them. I observe the shape and length of the cut of the vegetable as being bite-sized. I notice the way cutlery is laid out—straight and in proper order. I thank them for their assistance and note how easy dinner preparation was with their help. I point out simply what is true. They feel accomplished, noticed and appreciated. I comment on them doing homework, their speediness of getting going in the morning, their investment in their friends. I notice who they are, which is most obviously expressed in what they do. They know I care. When I am at my best, my interactions are positive and frequent, even through the mundane, everyday experiences of our shared lives.

Are there opportunities with your loved ones to increase the positivity in everyday ordinary activity? Seize it if you can. Your example, consistently given, will also significantly influence their behavior towards you.

Act kindly and politely

This point may seem obvious. Close loving relationships benefit from generosity and consistent civility. You know the expression "you catch more flies with honey than you do with vinegar". Yet, the benefit of kindness may be greater than you think. Yes, your kind actions may endear others to you; however, the research shows very clearly that your acts of kindness are their own reward to you! When you act kindly toward another person, you feel better about yourself. You feel not only love in your expression of generosity, but you have an appropriate surge of pride. This pride is both because you appreciate your own kind intention and also because your gift is real and meaningful to another.

When you act kindly, your self-esteem goes up. Your behavior is consistent with what you know are the better qualities of humanity. To be generous to others is an admirable action. We appreciate this so much that there are countless YouTube videos of people being nice to others. Why do millions of people watch these videos? Because simply witnessing kindness makes us feel good. Being kind is even more gratifying.

Positive interactions with your loved ones will increase with each kind act. Particularly pleasant and unexpected gestures may make a big emotional impact: flowers for no reason, or preparing someone's favorite dinner served on the best dishes. Actions like these may create a halo of positivity over an entire household for days. Surprisingly though, kindnesses that go unnoticed can also be powerful. If you act generously from your heart, as an expression of love, then you feel better even if your loved ones don't recognize the gift they received.

Increasing your own well-being by investing in your closest relationships is a certain winner. Few other happiness interventions are as well-founded in positive psychology research. Therefore, don't take your loved ones for granted. I moved to my current city to be closer to my mom and two of my siblings. I ensure that my two sons and I regularly spend time together. We eat family meals regularly—the kind where you sit around the table with no TV on. We plan activities on the weekends. We play cards. We hang out. My teenagers are so accustomed to this that I expect they don't often consider how out of step they are with many of their peers.

Give the most generous thing you can give to your loved ones. Give them your time. Commit to regular activities together. If there are strains in your relationships, time together is not an instant cure, but it's the surest way to truly cement a lasting committed bond.

If you don't yet have someone to love regularly in your life, have faith. Sometimes—always actually—life is in transition. Young adults moving to new cities often take intuitive actions. They call their moms often. They get a pet; loving your cat, dog, or other responsive mammal can be deeply rewarding. They connect with friends online and join clubs. Love, in varying degrees, is all around us. Humans are driven to it. Your loving actions will be reciprocated. The next chapter may have some helpful relationship-building ideas for you.

Points to Ponder:

- In what ways are you getting these feelings from your relationships: acceptance, support, caring, pride, fun and appreciation? What could you do to give these to others?

- How could your own routine interactions with the people you love be improved? Consider the mundane moments in your life. What opportunities are there?

14 Friends and Community

The Rat Race. We're all in it to some extent. Sometimes, we try to distance ourselves from it, but we participate in earning money, consuming goods, and scurrying about our busy lives along with everyone else. We work so we can consume. Fair enough. Why is it, however, that some people caught up in the Rat Race are themselves rats? Some folks play the game with a decidedly mean and selfish motive.

I've been guilty, on some past occasions, of playing this way too. Being a rat expresses itself both subtly and blatantly. I'm embarrassed that I've witnessed myself racing to a checkout lane in order to beat someone else and leave the store a couple of minutes faster. I've also criticized colleagues during a meeting in order to make myself look smarter. These kinds of behaviors do not win friends, and ideally would not influence people.

Moreover, the people I want to count as my friends ought to be kind, generous and motivated to be open "good" people. Conversely, I want my "goodness" to be my mainstay as I interact with others. This engagement of "good" people with other open "good" people is how the world generally operates. Thugs, bullies and tyrants find others like them to be with. Nice guys and heroes generally find the company of people who are also on the side of angels. We are attracted to people who are sufficiently like us.

Sabotage to our identity and our circle of friends is, however, lurking at every corner. Strangers and mere acquaintances have more influence on us than we think. Researchers Nicholas Christakis and James Fowler have shown that an individual's behavior cascades influence on the behavior of others. Not only might my best friend's interests influence me, but my best friend's interests influence my friends, my friend's friends, and even my friend's friend's friends. Everything people do influences others to at least three degrees of separation. So weight gain by someone doesn't just influence immediate friends, associates and neighbors. This influence cascades to dozens, hundreds, and even thousands of people outside the immediate circle of people who actually bear witness to an event. This research holds up in numerous applications—smoking cessation, happiness, exercise and weight control, and even politics. We are constantly bombarded with influences on our behavior that we are unaware of. And, we are influencing many more people than just those with whom we directly connect[1].

Equally fascinating sociology research shows that we have a profound and consistent bias against admitting to the influence of mass media. A much-studied phenomena called the "Third-Person Effect" shows that when asked, people deny incorporating or being influenced by mass media (pop culture included). Yet, we overestimate its effect on others. Essentially, we protect our egos by denying the effect strangers have on us, including the deliberate efforts of advertisers.

What does this mean? Whether we see it or not, we are subject to considerable influence from behavior changes of people who are strangers to us. We are in denial, or ignorance, about this effect. Additionally, mass media constantly bombards us with the message of the Rat Race: consume and get ahead at any cost. We deny this effect on our behaviors too. How do we combat these unwanted and personally unintended influences on our own behaviors so we can create a life of our own choosing?

First, we must be aware of, and admit to, the reality of our cultural and social immersion. It has profound and mostly unnoticed impacts on our thinking and our behavior. Secondly, we choose our media consumption. For example, turning off the TV and limiting our time surfing the web are effective actions. Finally, we choose our circle of friends, workmates, and to a large extent, neighbors.

It's been well-documented in positive psychology literature that happy people—those who report the highest levels of subjective well-being—are disproportionately members of a faith group; that is, they go to a church, synagogue or

---

1   If the effects of social contagion fascinate you as it does me, read "Connected: The Surprising Power of Social Networks and How They Shape our Lives" by Christakis and Fowler.

Mind: Mental And Emotional Happiness

temple regularly. I'm not necessarily advocating for this; however, for readers who do or did attend such group services, you will note that, in general, the people gathered there had good intentions toward the other people in attendance. Sure, some people saw themselves as superior and others gossiped. Still others cheated on their taxes or had elicit affairs. But by and large, most faith-based groups gather with a deliberate intention of being loving and supportive of one another. And despite the myriad human foibles that are present in every group, most people report positive experiences in such communities. No wonder they report higher levels of personal happiness.

What can we learn from this? The people we choose to have around us are VERY important. Communities—faith-based, work, neighborhoods, clubs—profoundly impact the quality of our lives. When we carefully choose who we spend our time with—to the extent that's possible—we have greater control over our social experience. Our emotions are, in part, a function of the climates we live in. Groups of people invariably create their own emotional weather patterns. Some groups are sunny and inviting and others are stormy and threatening. You can exercise choice over much of the climate you live in.

Communities profoundly impact the quality of our lives.

If your workplace is toxic, you can leave it. Of course, this is difficult and I don't dismiss the serious consequences of leaving work and finding a new source of income. However, your life and the quality of your daily experience is very important. You may want to believe that you can rise above the toxic work culture and be unaffected by it. Some can achieve this but most can't. Remember, we are greatly influenced by others and are generally in denial of this fact. It's difficult to resist the effects of a workplace poisoned by negativity and lapsed ethical standards. Get out if you can. Even small work groups that unite to push a better agenda often lose if the institution is big and the culture is well-ingrained.

Similarly, the neighborhood you live in is a choice. If you look around and see deterioration and social disorder, get out. It's bigger than you and it creates the emotional weather you live in daily. I've worked with people who are in helping professions and they sometimes argue that they are needed in these deleterious communities. Indeed, they are. However, where possible, I recommend that people live apart from unhealthy social environments. Then you can go to work, give yourself to the task of creating improvement, and when your work is done retreat to a haven that resuscitates your own energy, compassion and good will. Burn out, also know as compassion fatigue, plagues many helping professionals. These workers need safe, supportive communities as much as, if not more than, others.

Where you work, where you live and the family members who occupy your home are often communities we feel we have less choice about. But even in these areas we do have choices. We always have choices. The circle of friends and acquaintances we keep are squarely within our control. Are you fed positive energy by your friends? Do the people you spend time with encourage and support you? Are they, as a collective group, growing in a way that makes themselves and the world a better place? If you answer "yes" to these questions, rejoice! You are amongst people who are genuinely making you better.

By contrast, are your friends or other communities filled with negativity and complaint? Is this group's collective energy diminishing the collective well-being? If this is the case, then you have some work ahead of you. The easiest choice is often to give your time and energy to people who are inspiring, encouraging and kind. Alternatively, if you know you have substantial influence within your group, you can try to change the dynamic from within. More than anything, refuse to engage in negative complaining and gossiping. When your friends engage in it, don't participate in the conversation and try to change the topic. Some might ask why you seem quiet. Be honest. Tell them you want to create positive environments for yourself and others. Explain that you are choosing not to complain or focus on things that are less than perfect. You will probably be pleasantly surprised what good conversations flow from this. Regardless of what happens, hold your ground. If your friends can't or won't change, reach out to find new ones. Your commitment to be positive will make you much more attractive to others; the research strongly supports this. Positive people behave friendlier than others and, in fact, become more desirable to others.

When you are considering how to find good people to be with, consider your faith-based community. If you have a religious background or presently attend church (temple, synagogue, etc.), consider investing a lot of your social time within this group. You are likely to be rewarded with caring, positive friends who are committed to something more than meeting their own personal needs.

If faith-based groups are not your thing, consider joining the many other service-oriented clubs—Rotary, Lions, Elks, Kiwanis, and many others. Search through MeetUp.com and look at what's going on in your city. There are groups for people interested in politics, recreation, philosophy, health and well-being, alternative spirituality, environmental causes...you name it. Most organized groups have an operating assumption that members are well-intended toward one another. Naturally, there are other places where you can connect with good people. Even many online communities are doing wonderful work with genuine care and commitment for their membership. I have a bias toward face-to-face connections, but I don't discount the experiences of others who enjoy great relationships online.

To summarize, we are powerfully changed for better or worse by all kinds of social forces of which we are hardly aware. Your personal intentionality is the force by which social influences can be slanted in favor of your own happiness and growth. Your intentions, followed by your actions, to be with kind, upbeat people, makes a world of difference to the overall quality of your life. Volunteer to be a good friend to others and insist that your friends operate ethically, cheerfully and kindly toward you.

Points to ponder:

- What media are you consuming and what emotional tone does it carry? Noting that we generally deny the impact of third parties on us, what honest assessment can you make on the impact your media choices have on you?

- How are your friends helping you grow and be happy? What could you do to get more "good" and less "bad" from your social network?

15 Belonging to Your Tribe

Given that humans have evolved over the last million years to our present state, it's in a mere blink of an eye that we have lived in "modern" civilizations. Cities and countries are just a few thousand years old. All our history before 8,000 to 10,000 years ago consisted of tribal communities. This form of social structure provided exceptionally supportive environments for its members. Tribes rarely grew to more than a thousand members and commonly were much smaller. Members of a tribe were generally kin—connected by blood or marriage. Importantly, the tribe had a powerful driving principle: success as an individual was dependent on the success of the group. While pecking orders and competition within a group was expected, a logical limit on these behaviors implicitly governed against extremes. No one could be tolerated to strive for his own advantage to an extent that it put the tribe's existential well-being at risk. Such members who behaved beyond this limit would face swift correction or ultimately be rejected by the tribe. Consequently, tribes had a rhythm that allowed personal expression while maintaining collective responsibility. The overall effort of the tribe toward survival, harmony and growth (procreation) was reflected in the personal behaviors and motivations of each of its individual members. Individuals began to develop specialized skills to serve a community of other developing specialists. Some members cared for children, others were best at making baskets, others were hunters and others preserved food.

I don't want to be overly romantic about days gone by. Undoubtedly, some tribes imploded due to internal strife and selfishness. As well, inter-tribal warfare clearly is a part of our heritage. However, on the whole, a tribe was a community that holistically strived for its collective success. Knitted closely together by family relationships, genuine care and affection for other tribal members would have been the norm. As well, given that tribal communities generally numbered less than a thousand individuals, all members of the tribe would have a degree of relationship with every individual within the tribe.

Pro-social behavior is hard-wired into us. Our evolutionary development has primarily occurred in tribal settings over millennia; and not during our relatively short period of "modernity". Individual actions that add to cohesion and mutual support—lead to more success individually and within the tribe. Put simply, being kind and considerate served for greater reproductive success for the entire community. We know that we feel emotionally rewarded when we engage in pro-social behaviors.

Researchers can demonstrate this evolutionary bias. Among other studies, there is one that illustrates the point exceptionally well. Dunn, Aknin and Norton gave some students money to spend on themselves and other students money to spend on others. The researchers predicted that students spending the money on themselves would increase their happiness and that this would be much more true than spending the money on others. However, the opposite was true. Much higher, subjective reports of well-being were consistently reported when the money was spent on others. This same research has been done in several different international settings with identical results. Scientists even observe clear emotional rewards in toddlers who love to gift things to others. Pro-social behaviors—being kind and considerate to others—is a biological survival mechanism for our species. It helps with our collective survival. Nature's way of ensuring we engage in pro-social acts is to make us feel really good when we do it.

In tribes, pro-social behavior was rewarded with more than an infusion of happy, warm feelings. Because tribes were small and its members were closely relating with one another every day, pro-social behaviors were constantly being reciprocated. Today, I gathered roots and you ate. Tomorrow, you successfully hunt meat and I will eat. My wound needs binding and you help me. Your child is lost and I find her. Our interests, collectively and over the long run, are mutually supportive. Kind, thoughtful, generous behavior is constantly rewarded. Selfishness was likely relatively rare—consider Inuit elders who were known to suicidally leave their tribe when they could no longer make positive contributions to the survival of upcoming generations. While extreme, this demonstrates the profound focus on enduring pro-social behaviors.

You may be thinking this has nothing to do with how we live today given that we live in disconnected, massive social environments. Some of us are in cities with millions of individuals. And even for the minority who live in rural environments, few would describe their existence as anything like tribal kinship. Our western society, when looked at from its fundamental economics, is a parade of tragedies: violent crime, greedy corporations, environmental degradation, rampant consumerism and mindless pleasure seeking. In short, we have become detached from the "mutualism" that characterized tribal life. Instead, our ethos is largely self-seeking. "What behaviors work to my personal advantage? And to hell with anyone else's needs." Our economic and political rules reduce us to caring for very few others. Individualist motivations are the norm. At best, our society expects us to look after our children in addition to ourselves. At worst, fathers abandon their offspring in huge numbers and many mothers become pregnant when they are too young and have too few resources to capably raise children. This state of affairs feels so discouraging because it's alienating people from their own nature. But there are hints of our tribal nature in ordinary folks who are managing to live in direct confrontation to our western economic ethos. All kinds of people, in small and grand ways, are making choices to live in community with others. They look in on their elderly neighbors, they make environmentally responsible product choices even when it costs more, they volunteer for political or charitable causes.

I'm not advocating for a political overthrow of our current way of life. Reforms are sought and promoted by many people with greater expertise than mine. What I do strongly advocate is for people to be happy. To do that, we need to feel a belonging that is greater than to our immediate family. We need emotional attachment to our communities. We want to be connected to people whose plight is intimately tied up in our own. The tricky part in this is defining the size and composition of the group of people with whom we share a mutual interest in prosperity, peace and sustainability. People who live next door and in my block clearly share some of my interests. So do all the people who are paying the same municipal taxes that I do. The unemployment rate is one of the many shared concerns of my region. My country has created connections and interdependencies amongst all of its citizens. Wars, poverty and

We need to feel a belonging that is greater than to our immediate family.

pollution are just some of my connections to the global community. Air and oceans give me a direct visceral connection to the whole world.

Depending on your ethnic heritage, you lost tribal lifestyles from one or two generations ago to more than 100 generations ago. Nevertheless, all readers of this book now belong to myriad tribe-like social structures, from neighborhoods to global institutions. Our collective interest is to return to the ethos of tribal belonging. When we see everyone's basic concerns as entangled with our own, we come close to a global identity. When each individual's needs for physical and emotional security are recognized as interdependent with my own needs for security, then we have reclaimed our tribal membership.

However, we can't contribute to all people's needs, nor can we even begin to know them all. Like tribes of old, individuals must specialize to make a meaningful contribution. Perhaps your passion is neighborhood renewal, in which case you will organize block parties, write letters to your local government and generally contribute to your immediate neighbor's well-being. Another passion may be serving the homeless. Perhaps you volunteer at a soup kitchen and donate to charities. Someone else is working to stop over-fishing in the world's oceans. They give resources of time and money to eco-activist organizations. Perhaps they are advocating for political reforms. The needs of the global tribe are so many. What is your passion? What is the gift you can give? What specialized effort of yours connects you to our global tribe?

Do whatever you choose not only because it's right, not just because it makes a positive and much-needed contribution to humanity, but because it will reward you with surges of warm, satisfied emotions. Belonging to a community is your evolutionary necessity. When we are living out of step with this part of our nature, we are less happy. No matter what your cause is, make sure it connects you to other people. Be aware that this expression of belonging doesn't require any socially organized group effort.

I recall some years ago stopping an automatic donation to a well-known charity. What caused me to cancel my automatic payments was the ceaseless impersonal appeals for more money. Letters could be easily discarded, but even after several requests that the charity not phone me at home, I grew fed up and ended my support.

An unexpected dilemma arose. I still wanted to give away the amount of money that had previously gone to this particular charity. At about the same time,

I learned about the benefits of pro-social spending—how buying something for others feels good. I recognized that I had never gotten warm, fuzzy feelings when my bank statement came and I saw the automatic withdrawals that had gone out the past month to charities. So I decided I would say "yes" to circumstances that came into my life where others needed something that I could give. Of course, it didn't take long for an opportunity to arise. I was in a line at a sandwich shop, waiting for my turn to order. In front of me was a young couple—high school students—who were discussing what they could buy for the $10 they had between them. Of course, each sandwich on the menu board cost $8 or more. As I stood behind them, they became self-conscious that their discussion was delaying my ability to get lunch. With an embarrassed courtesy, they excused themselves and retreated several feet behind me so I could order. I did so, but I asked the cashier to add an extra $10 for the kids behind me. I got my sandwich and left. How did I feel? Elated! It was a small gesture, but I really liked helping some strangers who expected nothing from me. Spontaneous, unreciprocated generosity feels great!

Belong to our tribe. Find a way to reach out beyond your immediate circle of friends. Share what you can. Contribute in ways that feel personal and important to your values. And whenever possible, play an active part in something. The science shows that your emotional rewards for personal, pro-social behaviors will bring happiness. And as long as your needs are being met, pro-social spending will give you more enjoyment than spending the money, time or energy on yourself.

Points to ponder:

- What tribes do you belong to? What are you getting from them? What are you giving and how could you give a wee bit more?

- Is there a social cause that you have a passion for? In what small way, could you become more connected to the tribe that is engaged in this cause?

16 Culture Connects Us

Forgive me for pointing out some of the negativity of dominant western culture in the previous chapter. I am going to argue for embracing culture in this chapter. Are we to avoid being swept up by the collective mentality? Avoid TV? Avoid web surfing? Avoid the untoward and unnoticed effects of our unhealthy neighborhoods? Avoid the behavioral influences perpetuated by strangers far removed from our physical location and awareness?

No, you can't and shouldn't avoid all these cultural realities. The message of the last chapter was to be aware that you are constantly receiving social signals about what to think and do. To counteract negative influences, you must exercise your deliberate choice to be with people who influence you toward growth and positivity. Behave pro-socially and seek others who are also kind and well-motivated toward others. This will brighten your everyday well-being. Being with good people always brightens the mood.

Separate from the direct and indirect influences of individual people is our broad culture. Culture is an amalgamation of many people's beliefs, traditions and art forms. We are immersed in culture wherever we go. Even when you sit quietly in your own home, culture is all around you: the construction of your home, the shape of your furniture, the clothes you are wearing, the pictures on your wall, and even the food in your fridge. In a typical day, the immersive experience of culture permeates everything we do. The behavior of car drivers or fellow bus riders is culturally specific. Customary greetings, handshakes and eye contact are all culturally determined. Billboards are designed within the confines of deterministic art forms. Music plays over store speakers. Your workplace has dozens of complex social norms that you just know because, like almost everyone else, you are living as a full participant in the culture. Let me illustrate.

Consider a typical office culture. When you see a colleague in passing, you behave differently during each encounter on a given day. On first crossing paths, you greet each other with a "Hi, how's it going?" On a second encounter, you nod and smile. Perhaps on the third encounter, there is merely enough eye contact to be sure you do not crash into one another. How easily we navigate these complex behaviors without thinking. Imagine you have arrived from outer space and needed to figure it all out. Would you know to shake hands with the first person who offers to show you around? Would you then introduce yourself to everyone on the bus? Would you know how to dance? If you did know how to dance, would you dance to the music played in the store?

Culture is everywhere and it permeates all of our thoughts and actions. We even dream in culturally contextualized environments. This is breathtakingly wonderful and yet terrifying at the same time. Wonderful, of course, because even when we are alone, the collective pulse of our society embraces us; we have a sense of belonging and existential understanding by simply being in our familiar culture. It is also terrifying and absurd. I light-heartedly shudder to think that we may see a resurgence of leg warmers from the 80s. Fashion is fun, but it also enslaves us. I count the small blessings of being a man in this regard. Men's styles are a bit easier to keep up with. If fashion seems trivial, culture is also terrifying because America doesn't really question its warrior identity. Spending on combat and the tools of combat is simply a way of collective life. The presence of enough nuclear weaponry to destroy all human life twice over is something few of us pause to consider. At the same time, mainstream music that regards women as whores and objects plays idly in the background as children accompany their parents to the mall. The war on drugs and the resulting highest incarceration rate in the history of the world is another facet of culture. Culture can indeed be frightening.

How, then, do we navigate through and within a cultural framework so as to maximize our benefit? How can we soak up the best of our culture and protect ourselves from the worst? Awareness is the key. To what extent can we stop drifting like flotsam in the ocean, simply moving with the current, bobbing and submerging without any control over the water that envelops us? To make culture a wonderful contributor to our well-being, we first need to see it in our lives. Once we see it, we can choose and direct our experience.

When I played hockey for several years, I often considered the sub-culture that came with the sport. Men's recreational hockey is called the "beer league" for a reason. Many of my teammates drank heavily after each game. Coolers full of beer came to every game. Usually, the same few guys were the last to leave the dressing room and their departure only occurred when the cooler was empty. A host of problems were fueled by this cultural association of beer and hockey: they drove drunk, their families were ignored, they were often overweight, and they spent a small fortune on their habit. I thought it peculiar that this association was so deeply rooted. On different days of the week and over many years, I played with a number of teams. The association was constant. Some teams drank more or less, but even some players from my 6:30 a.m. drop-in group had beers following each game. We have collectively endorsed this subculture, its beliefs and its behaviors.

Are there cultural incongruences in your life that are contrary to your values? If so, can you eliminate or lessen their presence in your life? Does your media consumption lift you up and make you feel, think and act as you want to or does its negativity and shock value leave you mesmerized and deadened? Is the music you listen to beautiful and inspiring? When you look at the pictures on your walls, do they bring calm and infuse you with their beauty? Do they stimulate your imagination toward cheerful, pleasant subjects?

This kind of examination of the cultural influences affecting you holds much promise. Simply put, there are three kinds of influences: negative, neutral and positive. Cultural influences that are negative may be relatively easy to identify; however, they aren't always easy to walk away from. In fact, we often choose art forms that evoke disgust, shock and fear. Horror movies, many typical song lyrics and Mixed Martial Arts fights are but a few examples of the kind of entertainment prevalent in society. Negative, blunt emotional messages shock our middle brains. They can make us feel more alive momentarily, yet nothing good can come from this form of culture if we habituate to it. We will feel bad and suffer the emotional and physical consequences. It's unlikely to draw us to personal growth. Instead, a world filled with negativity regresses to simple, selfish survival instincts.

Neutral cultural influences may be agreeable. We may like the combination of color, texture and geometric patterns on a typical modern painting. Its abstract content, however, is perhaps unlikely to stimulate positive feelings. As well, for most of us, it does not stimulate our thoughts and dreams. As a source of energy, it may be inert; it gives very little to the observer.

Positive cultural forms are recognizable by the way they make you feel. You know their influence is good when your emotional resonance is deep. Art—music, philosophy, theatrical production, etc.—ought to draw us to our own expression of creative growth. This is not the same for each of us, thank goodness. If it were, the world would be boring. I believe culture is a tool at our disposal. We are not flotsam, captive to an ocean of popular culture. Rather, we can be fishermen, taking what nourishes us.

It's tempting to try to be specific in my views about what constitutes "good" culture, but I can't. It's too variable and constantly changing. Culture, by its nature, speaks in its time and to its community. My advice is to be aware that you are a consumer. Sample culture broadly; listen to many genres of music, learn to prepare food from many ethnic traditions, go to art galleries, museums and live performances. Travel broadly if you can afford to do so. And if you can't, wander around the ethnic enclaves of the nearest city. Seek out and pay attention to street performers. Go to a comedy club. Dance all around your house with the music good and loud. Take a class. Go to a busy park and watch the people there. Savor these experiences.

With your awareness tuned to what lifts you and enriches your life, you will come to identify styles and elements of culture that give meaning to you.

I will close this chapter with a brief anecdote. A few years ago I had the great pleasure of traveling in France and Italy for several weeks with my then-spouse and two sons (12 and 15 years old at the time). Naturally, we were spending a lot of time in museums, ancient ruins and breathtaking cathedrals. One day, we found ourselves surrounded by the ornate décor of the Museums of Strada Nuova in Genoa. These three palaces, at one time, were home to some of the richest bankers in all of Europe. Their exquisite 16th century architecture is itself stunning, but the treat is inside the large stately rooms, frescoed halls and interior courtyards. Although we had walked through many art galleries before, I recall being overwhelmed by an exhibit of Flemish painter Anthony Van Dyck's work. His sincere affection for his subjects so poignantly comes alive on his canvasses. Rich, textured oil paints portray humanity in both its suffering and its greatest triumphs. For no particular reason, tears began to well in my eyes. With an embarrassed grin, I allowed myself to breathe it in: beauty, glory, service to God and countrymen. While witnessing these ascendant qualities, I also saw the subjects as tender, vulnerable human beings just like me. Art capturing humanity at its finest. It works for me!

Points to Ponder:

- What facets of culture lift you and make your spirits soar?
- What new cultural experience do you want to try? How can you make it happen?

PART THREE

Spirit

The spiritual principals discussed in the following pages are not associated with a particular dogma—no specific religion or set of beliefs. My use of the word spiritual is a function of language; I think it's the right word. However, I know that we commonly associate spirituality with religion. If you have a particular religious doctrine that is meaningful to you, you may find your spirituality within the context of that doctrine. However, if you don't hold any particular religious doctrine as meaningful, you can still fully embrace and enjoy the spiritual life described in this section of the book.

Let's explore the aspects of spirituality that give our lives meaning, purpose and inner calm.

My own journey to spirituality has had several detours. I was raised in a Christian home and my family attended church regularly. In spite of the fact that I showed up and was an active participant, my perception was mostly that God did not do his part. He didn't show up. At least, he didn't show up in the ways I thought he ought to. My God, I was taught, performed miracles, answered prayers audibly, and guided the universe in a way that generally had direct benefit for the faithful. I didn't see any of that, despite my earnest prayers for an experience of divine power. Like many others, I left the church in my late teenage years. When I did attend a service, it was a ritual with little meaning. I still appreciated the community and the shared connection, but I didn't see God there. As a young adult seeking spiritual sustenance, I made real and protracted efforts of trying to find God in different churches and denominations, but I found the varying dogmas did not adequately feed my soul.

Ask me today if I know God and I would say yes, but I don't believe God is a singular, supernatural, omniscient powerhouse. My idea of God includes a source of enlightenment, amazement and enrichment, with which I do cultivate a personal relationship. And if this personal God speaks to me, it's in very subtle ways. As well as this personal God, I believe there is a totality of creation so astonishingly large and bewildering that it, too, is God. This God is awesome in the truest sense of the word. I am in jaw-dropping awe of the beauty and creativity of nature. I am amazed at the majesty of creation. I marvel at the size of the universe and the gargantuan power found within it. As I contemplate this universal, awesome God, I am stunned to see its nature reflected back in my small, short life. I know I'm made up of atoms that originated from the Big Bang 14 billion years ago. Somehow, these building blocks travelled through eons of time and over a vast distance to make me. And though I pale in comparison to the whole universe, I, too, am capable of creativity and beauty. I can give life and shape to it. I can graciously serve another as his life fades away. I am humbled by these powers and invigorated at the same time.

Whether a person believes in Allah, Jesus, Buddha, Krishna, Shiva, Bahá'u'lláh, Yahweh or no God at all, there are universal moments in life when we realize something that's greater than ourselves—these include when we are awestruck by nature, bowled over by love or pleasantly humbled by a recognition of our own insignificance relative to the universe. This capacity to see beyond our own egos is part of our humanity, a gift we are all endowed with.

Spiritual richness is, in some ways, hard to describe in words because it's an experiential truth. With no experience of it, the ideas and practices will be difficult to comprehend. Fortunately, all of us have touchstones that reveal to us some level of spirituality; that is, a realization of something sacred. This section of the book will help you connect to your spiritual self. I invite you to explore your childhood sense of wonder and consider how you can experience this again at a mature, meaningful level.

Fortunately, your happiness is not dependent on a perfect spiritual depth and awareness. Like going to the gym to work on your body, spiritual practice is merely a series of actions that, when done regularly, will enrich your life immensely.

This part of the book covers five topics:

- Developing inner calm and control over one's own mind

- Connectivity with others and the entirety of the universe, of which we are a part
- Gratitude and positivity
- Service and selflessness
- Cultivation of quality character

17 Contemplation and Mindfulness

Mindfulness is a wellness term that is in fashion right now. Mindfulness training and mindfulness activities are everywhere. But what is it? And how is it different from other kinds of contemplation. Most importantly, what's the big deal? Why is mindfulness so popular at this time?

Mindfulness is the practice of drawing one's awareness to what is happening in the present moment. With practice, it's the power to focus one's attention on a singular phenomenon; that is, an event that's actually happening, which can include thoughts occurring in your mind. As well, with practice, it's the power to be equally aware of all phenomena that are happening. One can hear the wind, see the leaves moving, smell the air and feel the breeze cooling the skin simultaneously, and experience it without thought or interpretation. Mindfulness is what we experience frequently in everyday life without effort or expectation on our part. Flow is an experience of mindfulness, when we are concentrated on a task that stretches our skill and little or no distraction draws the attention away. This experience is, if you will, "accidental mindfulness" and we know with certainty that flow is one of the most satisfactory states of consciousness we can experience. People consistently report happiness as a result of voluntary flow activities. Not surprisingly then, learning to be mindful on a more consistent basis and at will has tremendous personal benefit to our overall well-being.

No professional can claim more credit for the current mindfulness movement than Dr. Jon Kabat-Zinn. He is a professor of medicine at the University of Massachusetts. Through his research and that of others, he discovered that mindfulness can be a tremendous boost to health for people suffering from anxiety, stress, pain and illness. He found that mindfulness greatly assisted them. Unlike most western medicine, which is a trade-off between harmful side effects and expected benefits, mindfulness is purely healthful. It has no negative aspects. It assists people in overcoming disease both physically and mentally. Beyond that, it helps healthy people become even stronger both physically and emotionally.

Dr. Kabat-Zinn is the creator of a formal teaching methodology for mindfulness—MBSR (Mindfulness-Based Stress Reduction). It's fair to say it is taking the medical world by storm. But what's even more exciting is that it's taking the whole western world by storm. Fortune 500 companies are investing in mindfulness training. Teachers are learning how to bring mindfulness practice into classrooms. And community centers everywhere are offering workshops so anyone can learn mindfulness techniques.

So how do we get some of this magic for ourselves? First, let's take some of the mystique out of it. Mindfulness is a secular name given to ancient practices found in every major spiritual tradition. Christian and Sufi mystics may have had their own techniques to achieve harmonious, intensely focused states of consciousness. Similarly, traditional Shamanic healers used their unique methods to channel their focus very narrowly. In the East, meditation techniques have been practiced for thousands of years. Modern mindfulness techniques are most clearly aligned with teachings from these Eastern traditions. Meditation and mindfulness are nearly synonymous, but meditation as a religious ritual has dogma and symbolism attached to it. Consequently, the mindfulness movement shed any religious connotations. Training is distilled to an essential form and its components. As well, mindfulness can be achieved with techniques that are not always considered meditative—from Yoga to Tai-Chi.

Before I discuss some of the basic aspects of mindfulness practice, I think it's necessary to emphasize its wide-ranging and potent effects. Mindfulness is shown empirically to have the following benefits:

- Greater calm and resilience to stress
- Improved clarity of thinking, including perceiving more problem-solving options
- Improved immune response—fewer colds and flus
- Reduced heart rate
- Better pain management

- Better sleep

- Enhanced sexual function

- Reduced depressive symptoms

- Lowered anxiety

- Improved working memory

- Elongation of sustained task focus

- Improved emotional regulation

- Enhanced self-esteem

- Reduced distractibility

- Quicker recovery from physical and emotional trauma

- Improved interpersonal relationships as a result of greater empathy and compassion

- Faster mental processing

Wow! Why wouldn't everyone practice mindfulness given all of these life-enhancing benefits?

There are many books, internet resources and teachers from which you can learn mindfulness. I will provide a bit of guidance here. Mindfulness is not a skill that, once learned, can be applied flawlessly from that moment forward. It's more of a commitment to a way of living. At its core, it's a daily practice of dedicating time and energy to mindfulness. This practice can take a variety of forms, but must be consistently present for a period of time every day. A regular practitioner will sometimes miss a single day, but in order to reap the benefits listed, sustained practice is essential.

I adopted mindfulness in the form of meditation more than 27 years ago. When I had my own small children, I fell out of the habit for a couple of years. One missed day eventually became several until one day I realized I was no longer a meditator. Over time, all the previously gained benefits melted away. At some point I realized that the losses due to not meditating profoundly diminished the quality of my life. My practice is strong now and I am grateful for it. Having experienced the loss of mindfulness benefits, I am now deeply committed to regular practice. My depth of mindfulness is proportionate to the amount and quality of practice I give to it.

Yoga and Tai-Chi are excellent body practices of mindfulness. If you are a kinesthetic learner (that is, if experience is best integrated through movement) then I recommend you learn a daily practice in these ancient Eastern traditions. They have an added benefit over meditative practices in that you get physical exercise at the same time as you train your thinking and emotional areas of the brain. If these aren't your cup of tea, learning some basic meditation practices is easy, although meditating can be challenging for even experienced practitioners.

Basic meditation

Wear loose fitting clothes and sit in a comfortable position. Sustaining a solid, well-balanced posture is essential. You may want to experiment with different positions. A chair with moderate cushioning is fine. If it's too soft, it will cause you to slouch. If you are short, place a cushion beneath your feet so your legs are solidly grounded. I prefer to sit on a cushion on my carpeted floor in a modified cross-legged position. The heels of my feet are lined up with my centre and drawn in close to my buttocks, one heel in front of the other.

Whether in a chair or on a cushion on the floor, a straight back is essential for sustained practice. While seated, imagine having a string tied to the center of the crown of your head. Imagine the string is gently pulled up and then released so the spine is straight and yet relaxed. For many people, it's most comfortable, and therefore sustainable, to lower the chin slightly.

Your hands can be face up or down on your legs, a little way back from your knees. Alternatively, one hand can cup and support the other hand in your lap, close to your body. You should be comfortable and well-balanced. If someone pushed you gently on the shoulder, you should remain solidly stable.

Relax the breath. Take a deep, slow breath in. Fill your lungs completely. Then breathe out slowly, taking one or two seconds longer to exhale compared to your inhalation.

Illustration courtesy of the Ventura Buddhist Center

Do this two to three times. Scan your body from head to toe. Release tension and allow yourself to be physically relaxed. Your face and head can hold a lot of unnoticed tension. Consider your forehead and allow the muscles to relax and the lines there to smooth out. If your eyes are closed—this is typically preferred for beginners— open them briefly, and as you shut them consciously allow them to fall very softly; allow the muscles to the sides and below your eyes to relax. Relax your mouth and jaw. Let go of tension in your scalp, ears and neck. Work your way down your body. Letting your shoulders drop, your mid and lower back can let go. Consider the front of your neck, chest and abdominal muscles. Release any tension there. Your buttocks should feel relaxed and deeply settled below you. Scan your legs and feet. Let go. This total body scan may take just a few moments or you may move through your body slowly and thoughtfully, with full awareness as you feel each part of your body and release its tension. The body scan is itself a meditative technique with many variations. There is a guided body scan meditation that I invite you to try on my website: www.HappinessExperts.ca/resources.

Now your body is solidly and comfortably ready to begin the sustained part of your practice. I offer three suggestions. What works best for one person may not be as useful for another. Experiment with these techniques to see which feels most relaxing and easy to sustain.

Breath meditation — The object of this technique is to become completely focused on your breathing as it happens. Your attention is placed entirely in the breath. You do not need to breathe in a particular way; after all, nothing is more natural than breathing. Your body knows how to do this with no willfulness on your part. Your job is to be aware of each incoming and outgoing breath. There are two common ways of following your breath. Pick whichever works best for you:

1. Feel the inhalation right at the front of your nostrils. Notice that, as you start to breathe in, the air entering your nostrils is cool and refreshing. As you breathe out, feel the warm exhalation as it leaves your body. Observe your breath in and out through your nose—cool and invigorating through the in-breath, warm and relaxing on the out-breath.

2. Put your awareness in your abdomen, just beneath your ribcage. With this technique, pay attention to the rise of your abdomen with each in-breath and its gentle fall with each out-breath. Your diaphragm gently lifts and falls. Feel your body breathing in and out, expanding and contracting.

With either breathing technique, be aware of the moment when your in-breath completes and just before your out-breath begins. Focus on your complete breathing cycle—at the nostrils or at the belly—in, stop, out, stop.

Your mind will invariably want to turn its attention to other topics. It wants to have more stimulation than just the breath. This is normal and regularly occurs during meditation for even the most skilled practitioners. When you become aware of thinking, gently let it go and return your focus to breathing. It may shock you to discover how short your attention span is when you begin. Don't be discouraged. You are training your mind. Becoming aware of your interrupting thoughts IS the practice. It is by seeing the mind that we discover its content and conduct. Thinking will happen. Let it go and refocus. "To do" lists will start processing in your mind. Let them go. Daydreaming about some future activity will happen. Let it go. Return your awareness to breathing. Agitation and a restlessness will interrupt your focus. Let them go. Thinking will even turn to doubt about what good, if any, your practice is doing. Become aware of these thoughts and then return to your focused breathing.

Mantra Meditation — The singular focus of mantra meditation is the repetition of a short phrase. This phrase can be as little as one syllable—very commonly "OM". Phrases of two to three syllables also work fine. The syllables can be nothing more than pleasing sounds—usually with strong vowel sounds that are receptive and open—"OM, AH, OM" is a lovely three-syllable combination. Equally effective is a phrase that is relaxing and affirming. Some people choose words that are encouraging and kind to oneself. You might try, "loving calm" or "gentle peace" or a phrase that has significance in your religious beliefs. Christians may use something like, "Jesus loves me" or "loving God" or "unto You". Any phrase that is pleasing in sound and has a calm, special meaning for you will work. Once you have chosen a phrase, stick with it for an entire meditation session.

When using a mantra meditation, some people repeat their phrase out loud. This tends to lead to a parched throat—an unnecessary distraction. I recommend either silent repetition or beginning with a softly spoken mantra that becomes silent in a minute or two. Focus all your attention on your phrase. Even if you are silent, "listen" intently to every aspect of the syllables continually repeating their expression.

Just like in breathing meditation, your mind will interrupt your focus. Becoming aware of these thoughts IS the practice. When you notice them, instead of being frustrated, permit yourself a moment of smug satisfaction. You noticed your thinking! You are successfully meditating. Now return to your mantra. You may have another interrupting thought only a second or two later. Don't indulge it. Once you are aware of your thinking, return to your practice.

Both breathing and mantra meditation are object focused. They are commonly used forms of cultivating mindfulness and most people can use them quite successfully. The third style of meditation I will introduce here is less common. Many people find it challenging. For a minority, however, it is preferable and "easier" than object-focused meditation.

Open Awareness Meditation — Humans are miraculously sentient beings who are perceiving, sensing and experiencing many phenomena throughout every moment of life. Our senses are omnipresent—seeing, smelling, tasting, feeling and listening all the time. We don't stop and start sensing as we wish; rather, smelling happens even when we are sleeping. Close your eyes and ask yourself what you see. Stay with it; what do you see? Even with your eyes closed, there is sensory perception from your eyes. If the room you are in is dark, your brain still senses input from your retina—darkness. Because we are constantly sensing "stuff"—the phenomena that make up our reality—we learn to tune out sense perceptions in order to focus more exclusively on a subject of interest. For example, if I am absorbed in painting a portrait, I will stop smelling the solvents in the paint. There may be music in the background or occasional cars driving by outside. Due to my focus on what I am seeing and what my hands are doing while applying paint to canvas, I become completely unaware of my other senses. However, if my model stops sitting quietly and asks about the name of the music in the background, my shift in consciousness completely re-engages my hearing sense.

I now become entirely aware of sound. Thinking is another phenomenon just like our senses. I can be unaware of my thinking, just like I become unaware of background music. Open awareness meditation is a practice that expands consciousness to all phenomena simultaneously, including thinking.

Thinking is another phenomenon just like our senses.

Once in a stable, comfortable posture and having checked the body for tension, allow your attention to take in whatever is happening. A sound arises—perhaps a bird calling. Simply be aware of the sound. No need to interpret it—don't ask what bird it was or what the call may have meant. Simply hear the bird call and then let it go. In the distance, a refrigerator condenser switches on. The gentle hum of this equipment enters your consciousness. Just hear it. No need to do anything more. This may be the whole practice—just listening to whatever arises—sound waves coming into your eardrums. There is no need to interpret or wonder about the sound. Just listen. Sounds come and sounds go. If thinking arises, and it will, notice it and then let the thought subside.

If you are able to expand awareness beyond your auditory sense, you can try this too: sitting comfortably with your eyes open, notice what is seen. Don't look around. Instead, pick a spot in the foreground, perhaps six to nine feet away, just below eye level. Observe without focus that light, shape and color are being sensed. Allow this experience to just happen. No need to interpret this sight. It just is. While seeing, you will hear a phenomena send sound waves to your ears. Just hear. Awareness of your hands resting on your knees may happen. This has a specific feeling to it—the fabric of your clothes, the temperature of your skin, the precise place of contact between your hand and cloth… Just notice. Just feel. There is nothing to do and no place to go. While you are doing open meditation, you are resting with all the phenomena. You feel yourself swallow saliva, you blink your eyes. Sounds, sights, thoughts…experience all phenomena equally and without interpretation just are as they are.

You are like a still body of water, endlessly receptive to whatever arises. Phenomena are like a gentle breeze. With a soft wind, the water has small rippling lines run across it. But then the wind (phenomena) ceases or changes in form, and different patterns now form on the surface of the water. The water itself is not, however, changing form. This is analogous to open awareness meditation. Phenomena arise and pass, and your awareness, like the water, is stable and consistent. Awareness is pure and simple, attuned to whatever is actually happening without judgment or interpretation.

All of these mind training techniques—breathing, mantra and open awareness meditation—lead to the same place. They provide a forum for cultivating calm awareness. Training exercised in formal practice carries forward to your normal activities of life. The calm state of mind and greater awareness of what is happening in the moment is what leads to the long list of benefits listed earlier. When we regularly practice meditation, we foster an ability to have heightened awareness of real things that are happening in our lives. We perceive better; we notice more detail in what we see, hear, taste, touch and smell. We become aware of the nearly constant chatter in our minds. The stronger your meditation practice, the greater your ability to be present in the actual moments of your day.

We can make rituals out of everyday life opportunities to practice growing skills of mindful awareness. When we apply calm awareness to everyday life, we experience it differently. And because our experience of the world is different, for us the world is different. Try some of these rituals of mindfulness:

- Eat your first bite of any food slowly, allowing a deep sensory experience of flavor, temperature and texture.

- Upon entering any doorway, pause for a moment to see fully who and what is in the room. What are you aware of? Who do you want to be now?

- Every time you wash your hands, consider your experience for just a moment. What do the slippery bubbles of soap feel like? Can you smell the soap? What is the temperature of the water? How do your hands feel as they rub over each other?

- As odd as it may sound, urinating and defecating are rich sensory experiences. Do you notice or are you busy thinking? Try taking in the experience fully. Mindfully appreciate your body.

- Before you begin your paid work, be fully in position and ready to proceed, then pause for one breath. Be fully aware of your lungs filling and emptying. If you notice your breath is short, take another, longer mindful breath. Your productivity and ease of work will be greatly improved.

- Add your own rituals to everyday life such that you can grow your mindfulness practice as a way of being.

The practice of formal mind training is the gold standard for well-being interventions. Hundreds of rigorous studies have been done on mindfulness and found that few interventions have as big or as profound an impact. It may take a bit of effort to learn a practice of formal mindfulness training, but it's so worth it. Your brain actually changes its natural neural networking. With regular meditation, the left pre-frontal cortex grows more powerful. This is shown on imaging taken with Functional Magnetic Resonance Imaging (fMRI). More neural pathways grow in the region of the brain associated with happiness and emotional contentment. A bit of meditation practice can literally rewire the brain to greater happiness.

How much meditation is necessary for this benefit? You don't need much, but more is better. Buddhist monks who have dedicated major portions of their lives to mindfulness training have been found to have distinct and potent neural pathways. Not only do they have strong left pre-frontal cortexes (the region housing contentment), but they can also turn their consciousness to compassion. When they focus on compassion, their brain images show exquisite neural networking in a different part of the brain that's known to be the seat of empathy. Moreover, when a well-trained mind is concentrated, only the called upon parts of the brain are active. Calm focus makes the brain a powerful servant of its master. Some monks tested in fMRI machines have had more than 10,000 hours of meditation training. Their results are stunning. However, college students with just eight weeks of training showed demonstrable change in their neural networks, and as a huge bonus they report a more cheerful, calm experience of life. Meditate for a minimum of 20 minutes every day. More is better.

One last word on mindful meditation and why, for me, it's the most important part of a spiritual life. Meditation is a tool to grow awareness. Most importantly, we can grow awareness of our thinking. For many people, thinking happens continuously without their awareness. If these people are lucky, their thinking will be optimistic and kind to them. But even in this fortunate circumstance, can these people truly master their own responses to the environment? Moreover, if thinking is happening in a generally negative pattern and without awareness, how will these less fortunate people respond to the phenomena that make up their lives?

By growing mindfulness within us, we expand our opportunity to be FREE. If we are unaware of our thoughts, we are their slaves. We feel otherwise, but truly we are not free. People who are unaware of their negative thinking believe their thoughts. A young woman may stand in front of a mirror—her svelte figure lovely to any objective third party—and tragically think, "I look fat in these jeans." This kind of constant chatter, which is happening in most people's heads, is often not our friend. A man going for a job interview may say to himself as he opens the door, "I always get really nervous at these interviews." Without an awareness of his thoughts, he will be victimized by them. It won't occur to him to script his thinking differently. Chatter about all manner of things constantly bombards most people's brains. Their moods and actions don't reflect who they want to be or what they want to do. Mindfulness training changes this.

Mindfulness creates a gap between the world around us—including the world of our own making within our minds—and the way we respond to it. We are always sensing phenomena and thinking, and then we respond to these inputs. For example, if I think I always get nervous at job interviews, I respond by physiologically becoming nervous. If someone cuts me off in traffic, I respond with anger. If my spouse does not compliment my new clothes, I may think I'm unattractive. We respond to our automatic thoughts. Our feelings and actions flow from this unconscious thinking. Mindfulness provides a space between the stimulus and the response. And in this space we can begin to choose our response.

Mindfulness provides a space between the stimulus and the response.

The man who is cut off in traffic may argue that his becoming angry is the natural and "right" response. He will argue that to choose another response may be ridiculous. The truth is that, without the space within which to choose a response, he simply isn't free to have any other reaction. With mindfulness training, this same man will feel the anger response begin to rise in him, but because of his awareness he can choose what comes next. Does he want to be angry, have his heart rate increase, drive more aggressively, and maybe even drive right up to the offending driver to honk his horn and shake his fist? If he were truly free to respond, most likely he would choose a different response. Perhaps he would note the license plate and call the police. He might wonder what pressure and stress the other driver must feel to cause him to drive so recklessly. Maybe then he would count his blessings.

Mindfulness lets us become aware of our thoughts and feelings and then choose how to work with them. It's a profoundly rich gift you can give to yourself. From a place of mindfulness, you are truly free to make the life you want. Within your spiritual domain, mindfulness is the practice by which you give meaning and purpose to every other part of your life. It makes you free.

I have been practicing for a great many years and I can't imagine ever going back to a life without the degree of freedom I have won through mindfulness.

I wish much awareness, peace and happiness for you.

Points to ponder:

- What, if any, practices in your life, give you a heightened awareness of the present moment? Can you build more of this practice into your life?

- If you don't have a practice, which options in this chapter look appealing to you? How can you introduce it into your life?

- How would more freedom to choose your thoughts, and be less reactive, change your everyday experience?

18 Contemplative Connection

In the same way mindfulness connects us to ourselves and what we most want to be, contemplation connects us to the world and how we want it to be. They are similar. The former is training for our inner being. The latter is engagement outside ourselves. When I am most calm there is very little gap between my inner being and my presence in an ever-changing universe. This chapter will try to unpack this idea of connecting ourselves with the sacred nature, and interconnectivity, of all things.

What is contemplative connection? Words cannot describe a relationship with, or a means to create a relationship with, an entity that is beyond words. Yet I hope that, even with the inherent limitations of language, every reader will feel and know what I am trying to describe.

Contemplative connection is the spoken or unspoken experience of reaching out to the infinite universe—giving and receiving. Ultimately, it's a felt experience of oneness with everything...connecting with an infinite universe...becoming one with it... It's not in my nature to say (or write) things that are so esoteric and potentially devoid of meaning for my audience, yet there it is. On some level it feels like a bunch of fairy dust and baloney. On another level it's the only thing that makes sense. To get it, to really understand it, to see the vastness of what I am trying to say, let's get to a metaphor of something small and simple.

I like preparing pizza from scratch. In some ways it's an act of love. I use wholesome, healthy ingredients and my family really enjoys eating it. Before the dough bakes or rises or takes any shape at all, I scoop flour from a large container. I scoop it by the cupful. Within each cup are individual, fine particles of flour: about seven billion particles per cup. If a bit of flour spills onto the countertop, and I look carefully, I can perceive an individual speck of flour. I sweep it off the counter and into the mixing bowl.

Where and how does that individual particle come to be a part of my supper? It came from a store where stockers put it on a shelf and a cashier put it into my shopping bag. A trucker drove it to the store from a warehouse. In the warehouse, people moved the flour from one place to the next using powerful forklifts. Before then, it was packaged at a mill along with thousands of tonnes of ground grain. The grain came by train from the central plains of North American farms. A farmer harvested the grain, but only after he planted a seed. Rain caused the seed to swell. And warmth from the sun gave energy for the seed to sprout. As it grew, bees drank nectar from its flowers and carried pollen from some other shaft of wheat. Only then could grain begin to form. Only with water and sunshine can these seeds mature to a more fruitful form. The warmth from the light of the sun travelled a breathtakingly far distance to reach the grain—it would take 19 years to fly non-stop all the way to the sun. The sun burst from the same explosion that created all that we know, the Big Bang. In human terms, the sun is incredibly far and yet it's so close in cosmic terms, it's proportionately our next door neighbor. The nearest galaxy to our own is 25,000 light years away, and there are trillions of galaxies. A particle of flour came from the same source as all those galaxies. So did you and I. If this isn't a mythical story of greatness, then I don't know what is. Yet this story is not a myth. It is our truth.

Most religions formed a contemplative connection through prayer. They imbued the power of the interconnected universe with some super-human form and then they prayed to this form. They expressed thanks for what they had and they sought out the direction from God(s) into the practical aspects of their everyday lives. And why not? Some power is surely moving, shaping and constantly shifting the world we live in. We all want to acknowledge this power and, to whatever extent is possible, we want to connect. It doesn't matter to me what form we try to conceptualize as the source of this power. Simply tune into it. It's real. And you are constantly subject to its effects.

I was inspired some years ago by the work of Ken Wilbur. He is a philosopher with a special interest in spirituality. He describes the ways we can relate to the source of all power—you can call it God if that word is meaningful and helpful to you. He noted we can be awestruck by the enormous universe we live in. We can sense the power and beauty of creation. We can see the universe as this source and sustenance of all life. We can be in a posture of reverence toward this universe. We can perceive its grandness and marvel that, in all its power, there is a place for our own life force. We also want the universe to behave in certain ways. We want to avoid catastrophic events and we desire good things: peace, love, money, etc. We know that the universe provides all things. Many of us then pray to the universe—God, if your prefer—as a personal entity that may serve our own life. As we consider this vast, incomprehensible total universe, we cannot conceive of an interpersonal relationship with it. For this reason, we have personified deities so we can relate the source of all things to our own short, cosmically insignificant lives. We revere the source and make it personal in some way so it matters both in its grand context and in the daily affairs of our own lives. We see the big, mighty source that can be in relationship to our own self, in our own time and place. There is still one more way we can relate to the source: we can see ourselves in our best form. We are creative, powerful, kind and loving. We are a reflection of the qualities of the universe. There is an echo of God within each of us. In summary, there are three ideas of this source:

We are a reflection of the qualities of the universe. There is an echo of God within each of us.

1. There is a universal source of all things.

2. There is a power we want to tie into; that is, have relationship with.

3. There is our own best self: beautiful and altruistic.

Through contemplative connection, we can relate to all three ideas. We do it by accident when we are struck by something magical and beautiful. We marvel at the universe when the beauty of nature penetrates our hearts. We become deeply grateful when "luck" bestows a meaningful gift upon us. And we swell with healthy pride and experience great joy when we perform a small gesture that makes a difference in the life of someone else. In these types of circumstances, we stumble upon our varied relationships with universal, relational and personal "holiness" (or connectivity with the source).

As every other part of this book has emphasized, it's about our own intentionality. In the context of this chapter, we can intentionally connect to the source. We do this through deliberate contemplation. We stop scurrying from task to task. We set aside time and space. We gently create a mental tone of reverence.

Prayer is, for many of us, a familiar practice of contemplation that helps us experience connectivity with the source. If prayer is a loaded word for you, call it "talking to yourself". It's a deliberate reflection on the beauty and power all around you. It's a deliberate engagement on a personal level with your place in the grandness of the universe. It's a deliberate and earnest consideration of your own character and how you can be of service to others.

My prayers, I am embarrassed to admit, are often convoluted and filled with digressing thoughts. I pray to no one and to God (whoever she is). I pray to my deceased dad (whom I never knew) and to my father-in-law (whose hand I held when he breathed his last). I pray to the universe as a whole. I simply don't know who better to pray to. Part of me fully accepts that I may be praying to myself as a way to become grounded in forces so much bigger and grander than any I encounter in my ordinary life.

When I am somewhat perfunctory—as I often am during my morning routine of prayer, gratitude and meditation—my prayer often sounds something like this:

Here I am God, consciously with you. You are beautiful and powerful. Thank you for the nature I see out my window. Its abundance and constant growth astound me. The air I breathe right now and the power of the universe are connected.

I am dedicated to my own harmonization with forces of goodness. I am respectful of others. I listen well. I am responsible to the environment. I am sincere and honest. I am gentle and kind. I do no harm to others. I am supportive and of service to all people and all things. Give me today the things I need. Thank you for the stunning riches I have.

Bless my family. (Here, I pray situationally for the things my loved ones need and want, and for things I need and want.)

May there be peace, fairness, and good stewardship on earth.

Thank you. Thank you. You are awesome.

The words I pray vary a lot, but the gist of it is often the same. It's my conscious effort to connect with the source. My prayer recognizes power and beauty. It compels personal responsibility to be in harmony with goodness. It asks for the universe to bestow the things we need and want.

After I pray I feel good. I know I'm inclining my future self towards behavior and motivations that are inherently life-giving and desirable. Contemplative connectivity is certainly a pathway to greater happiness.

Besides formal prayer, there are other good ways to taste and enjoy the power of the source:

- Reading books and articles that inspire you toward greater wisdom and wholesomeness is an excellent way to reflect on who you are within a reality that is much bigger than your ordinary life.

- Reflective writing: journalling directed toward positive reflection and inspired intentionality can be a powerful means of connecting to the source.

- Spending quiet time in nature, absorbing the peace and beauty around you, helps you to see peace and beauty within you.

- Creating and/or enjoying music and art can be tremendously uplifting when the craft is directed toward beauty, peace and love.

I strongly encourage readers to make a deliberate practice of some kind of contemplative connectivity. Along with my regular meditation practice, contemplation grounds me. It helps me be who I want to be. It sets direction for my future actions. It reminds me what goodness is and it primes me to create and receive goodness. Every day, first thing in the morning, I meditate and formally contemplate. One additional practice at this early morning hour lays the foundation for the rest of my day: gratitude.

Points to ponder:

- What is your belief in, and relationship to, a higher power?

- What daily investment are you making in connecting with this power source? How could you make this investment bigger and more powerful?

19 Gratitude

Thank you for reading so far into this book. It delights me to think readers are finding value in the words I have written. It sincerely rewards me to have you engaging with this subject matter. As I wrote this, I imagined happy future readers. Even before the book was published (or finished being written), I was grateful for the thought of an audience enjoying my work.

Gratitude is an odd sort of emotion. It's usually a bit lively and energizing. When you feel grateful, your eyes open wide and your tone of voice brightens. It's almost always cheerful. You become more open to the people around you. You smile. You are warm-hearted. Perhaps you are even humbled in a good way if you are grateful for a profound, unexpected kindness. You may even marvel—an experience of being awestruck—at the goodness of someone or something. When you are grateful, you are deeply acknowledging the abundance and nurturing qualities of the universe (God, if you prefer). Pause for a moment and consider a time when you were deeply grateful. Think of the details. What happened? Who was there? How did you feel?

Pause for a moment and consider a time when you were deeply grateful.

It's a nice feeling, isn't it?

There has been a tremendous amount of research done on the psychological and physiological effect of gratitude. You won't be surprised that there is overwhelming evidence of gratitude's profound benefits. These include:

- Greater happiness
- Less anxiety and more calm
- Reduced risk for heart disease
- Improved energy
- More financial and career success
- Increased empathy and selflessness
- Better decision making
- Increased resilience
- More and deeper friendships
- Better marriages

It's no wonder that every major spiritual tradition emphasizes gratitude.

Formal research studies show that subjects who are required to engage in simple gratitude practices experience much higher levels of happiness. A powerful and unexpected finding is that the increased levels of happiness are still detectible six months after subjects discontinued their gratitude practice. In the positive psychology literature, few interventions, if any, are as simple and as effective in boosting happiness as are gratitude practices. I will teach you a few techniques in this chapter. But first let's explore why truly grateful people are sometimes hard to find.

Evolution teaches hard lessons. Genes that don't improve chances of survival tend to die out. Our primitive ancestors were not well-equipped for survival. We have no fangs or claws. We are slow runners. And our fragile skin makes us susceptible to extreme weather. Our massive brains, however, made us very effective at avoiding threats. We became ultra sensitive to stimuli. Let me illustrate.

It's a lovely day among the tribal cave people[1]. There is Og, a young, cheerful member of the tribe. Og is extraordinarily optimistic and willing to try new things. Oh! There's a saber-toothed tiger on the edge of the forest. Og delights in its beauty. It looks warm and fuzzy. Og decides to wander over to see if he can get an opportunity to touch the tiger. Og never comes back. We will miss his cheerful ways. Then there is Og's cousin Tok. He, too, is very positive and embraces all

---

1   Credit to Joe Dispensa who tells a story much like this one. I am paraphrasing him.

experiences with equal enthusiasm. What's that? The neighboring tribe is rushing over the hill, coming directly toward Tok and his tribe. The visitors are running and they are carrying spears and rocks. Tok wonders why they are coming. He gets up and rushes out to greet them. Poor Tok. We'll miss him too.

Fortunately, Tok and Og's influence in the current gene pool is non-existent whereas the tribe members who were cautious about the tiger and the invading competitors survived. We inherited their genes. Sensitivity to negative stimuli is an important part of our heritage. If we survive the poison berry, the attack from a wild animal or the threat from war, we learn from the experience. This facet of evolution is referred to as our "Negativity Bias". It means we are impacted to a much greater extent by negative events than by positive ones. Survival requires this sensitivity. However, when survival is not at risk, we flourish when we are aware and take stock of the positives in our lives. In order to overcome the effect of the Negativity Bias, we need to counter with many more positives. Some interesting research by Marcial Losada[2] and Barbara Frederickson suggests that the magic ratio is three to one. That is, for every negative thought we need three positive ones to maintain a "happy" equilibrium. Without a three to one (or higher) ratio, we succumb to stress, low mood, less energy and less creativity; in other words, we don't enjoy the many benefits of positive emotion.

Thus, there is a large psychological—I would call it spiritual too—benefit from learning gratitude practices. These simple techniques directly enable anyone to increase their ratio of positive to negative experiences. If you want to bring peace to your heart, a skip to your step and a smile to your lips do one or more of these:

- Three good things a day — List what specific things went well in your day or what stood out for you as especially good. Write it on a note pad or type it into your smart phone. A quick and easy way for you to record three things you are grateful for is all you need. Add to your list every day. As with any good habit, do it at the same time every single day. This technique works because you are

---

2   Dr. Losada is a delightful man with whom I have enjoyed discussing positive to negative ratios. He has studied countless business teams and their interaction with one another. His team observations are extraordinarily detailed and precise. Amongst other things, he studies how team members discuss ideas: Are words positive or negative? Are people speaking with inquiry about another's ideas or advocacy for their own? He notes objective criteria for performance: profitability and customer service ratings for example. His research shows that three positives for every negative interaction indicates powerful team performance. Four to one is better and six to one leads to world class outcomes.

training your brain—creating neural pathways—to look for and recognize positive stimuli.

- Gratitude journal — Similar to the "three good things" exercise, this one is also a simple daily habit. It differs in that you are only recalling one good thing, and you are expansively considering the details of this good event or experience. Write down what the experience was. Who did what? What was said? Why did that experience happen? How did you feel? In a paragraph or two, you have a clear story of something that made you appreciate life, even if it's just a little bit more. As with the prior technique, the research demonstrates the effectiveness of training your mind to pay attention to and look for the good in your life.

- Letter of Gratitude — This powerful technique can be used in combination with the prior two, but I recommend it as a stand-alone practice. Here, you search your past, from early childhood all the way to present day. Search for experiences that were especially meaningful, perhaps life changing. Can you see a person who was a big part of the event? Perhaps a parent, friend, school teacher or boss. Once you have identified someone who was instrumental in bringing about an experience that was especially meaningful, write that person a letter. Tell them what the experience was, how they made it happen, and the effect it had on you. It may not be appropriate or possible to share your letter with the person, but if it is, send them your hand-written letter. Better yet, arrange to meet with them, read the letter and present it to them. This can be a powerful experience both for you and for the recipient. Just as some negative stimuli are more potent than others, this letter-writing technique packs a big punch of positivity. Because it cannot form a daily habit, I recommend it complement one of the two previously described gratitude practices.

Gratitude practice has changed my experience of life in profound ways. I am friendlier, more outgoing and genuinely more cheerful. I see how fortunate I am. I count my blessings. In the rich, safe part of the world I live in, I recognize that I have few needs. I am kinder to others. I have greater confidence in pursuing my passions. I wake up looking forward to my day.

I am not recommending that anyone become a Pollyanna with an unrealistically positive view of the world. This just makes us cynical in the end. I acknowledge and accept the negative emotions that come with bad experiences. But I also actively attend to the many good things in my life. These positive people, places, things—blessings—in my life are real. I don't want to fail to see them. I want to love and embrace them. The more you practice gratitude, the more the universe unfolds opportunities for you. I am not suggesting this in some magical way. The universe is always providing opportunities, but when negativity is in charge of our lives, we fail to see the blessings within our reach.

Practice gratitude. Love what is lovable. Tending to these states of our heart makes them grow!

Points to ponder:

- In what ways do you see the good in your life? Do you have rituals or daily practices through which you consciously acknowledge what is going well for you?

- How can you incorporate more gratitude into your life?

20 Cultivation of Quality Character

"Happiness is secured through virtue;
it is a good attained by man's own will."

- Thomas Aquinas

Quality character. It seems like a quaint, old-fashioned notion. We don't talk about it much these days. I expect this is because, at a time not so long ago—100 years perhaps—the idea of quality character was narrowly defined. Society generally had an aversion to individuality. Conformity and regimentation was seen as a social good. Religious and socially conservative people laid claim to what constituted good character. As a result, if you weren't like them, then your character was suspect.

Powerfully, a counter-cultural movement took hold in the west during the 1960s. The ideals were about love and peace. Free expression and social activism were valued. Unfortunately, a damaging drug culture, irresponsible sexuality and self-absorption also accompanied this movement. This negative component diminished the movement's credibility when it came to speaking of character.

Today, we have generally accepted a "live and let live" view of morals and character: "As long as you don't impinge on my rights, you can be as you are." Most people have neither the ideals of the 1960s, nor the social conservatism that came before this time. Yet globalism, ecological imperatives and a maturing culture have begun to allow more time for a renewed discussion about quality character.

What, then, is quality character? This isn't easy to answer without falling into the trap of dogmatic, social moralizing. It's probably easier to agree on what is not quality character. Self-serving greed and lust are poison and we all see their destructive energy. Gluttony (insatiable appetite), be it for food, power, sex or fame, is repulsive. Irresponsible and excessive loss of emotional control is universally disdained—angry tirades and violence, which use fear as a leverage for power, are ugly. I could go on about negative character traits, but I prefer to offer some suggestions as to what constitutes universally admirable personality features.

Lao Tsu, an ancient Chinese philosopher, presents a simple picture of virtue. He describes four character traits that allow those who embody them to live spiritually contented lives. These four are described as follows:

1. **Loving respect** — This is recognition and appreciation for our own place amongst a universe of co-existing entities. With loving respect, I see other people as valuable and worthy of my best qualities. I listen well and I give maximum allowance for others' self-expression, up to the point at which my love and respect for myself are called into question. With loving respect, I see nature as a part of me, something to care for and protect. The natural environment is the ultimate source of awe. I see myself as a component part of nature. Just as I am nourished, warmed and cared for by nature, I return to it deep care.

> Loving respect recognizes the interconnection of all things.

Loving respect recognizes the interconnection of all things. It's continually grateful for this interplay of people, plants, animals and material things. To this degree, at minimum, loving respect is deeply spiritual. Another way to describe this virtue may be to simply say it is a life of reverence.

2. **Truthfulness** — Lao Tsu notes that honesty goes beyond speaking truth. Deep truthfulness is a sincerity in both words and actions. This virtue is the opposite of deceptive behaviors and compels us to avoid cheating of any kind.

Being truthful is about what's in our hearts. Playful teasing, genuine well-intended white lies and honest mistakes do NOT eliminate the quality of a true heart. A true heart gives freely what it owns: its knowledge, feelings and considered intentions. It can be trusted. The true heart consistently patterns actions that give rise to peace and confidence amongst friends, colleagues and lovers. This virtue requires truthfulness to one's own self too. We accept ourselves as we really are and from this place of truth, we can create our highest self.

3. Kind friendliness — Someone may be blessed with traits of loving respect and truthfulness, but still not give their warmest, most well-intended self to others. A character deficit exists. This third virtue fills the void. It is the quality of forging relationships founded in gentle well-wishing for the other. It is simple and unassuming.

When my personal agenda is always paramount, I am out of harmony with this virtue. When I'm committed to the cultivation of this character trait, I see my agenda as one harmonized with the needs and wants of the other.

Kind friendliness avoids harming others. It is gentle, warm and pleasant. Others are equal to one's self.

Everyone is worthy of kind friendliness toward oneself. Judgment and self-criticism are held in check with this virtue; a person is gentle, warm and pleasant to oneself.

4. Service — The fourth and final of Lao Tsu's virtues is service. This character trait is dedicated to creating and contributing to humanity and all ecology. It's expressed in gestures grand and small, from holding the door for strangers to leading a cause for social justice. Service is helpfulness. Our jobs, almost by default, are service-oriented. Assisting a child with homework, making a family dinner and helping a neighbor plant a tree are all actions that exemplify this virtue.

Service is our contribution to the universe. Kind friendliness is our disposition and manner. Truthfulness is the quality and condition of our heart. Loving respect is our recognition and appreciation of our place within an interconnected cosmos.

Many similar, perhaps more nuanced, lists of positive character traits could be made. I have an affection for the simplicity and completeness of Lao Tsu's list. You may have noted these four virtues in my daily prayer described in Chapter 18, Contemplative Connection.

The description of these four virtues contain enough detail to understand the intentions we want to create. They provide guidance for our aspirations. At the same time, I hope you see yourself in them—you, of course, already embody qualities of loving respect, truthfulness, kind friendliness, and service to self and others. Cultivating quality character is the desire followed by actions that make these four virtues a reliable and consistent expression of our being.

Remember Plato's Theory of Forms. We envision perfection and accept what really is, which is always something less than what the imagination can conjure up. This is also true for these virtues. If you have perfected those character traits, put down this book and come teach me. Few, if any of us, will live perfectly in the state of virtuosity described by Lao Tsu. The goal is to be aligned to these characteristics. You may want to repeat the four virtues at least once a day. State them as though they are already a condition of your character. With regard to the first virtue say, "I am loving and respectful. I am a spiritual being, deeply connected to the universe. I am a good listener. I am sensitive to, and supportive of, my place in all of ecology." This prayer affirms what you wish to be as though it was already true. You can pray similarly for the other three virtues, claiming them as your own every day as part of your contemplation practice.

When I am out of alignment with these desired virtues—if I am angry, judgmental, selfish, etc.—I usually feel the sting of it. Pain helps me to see and appreciate the need to get back on track to be a better person. I want to be a positive, contributing being in the universe. I want it every bit as much for how good it makes me feel as for the wholesome, beneficial energy it gives to the world.

Aspiring to live in alignment with quality character traits is different from wishing for these virtues. Meditation and prayerful contemplation are really just school for the real life that follows. I try to begin everyday with quiet schooling. I direct my intentions toward how I want to be. Then, of course, real life happens. My kids dawdle while getting ready for school. A driver cuts me off in traffic and scares the heck out of me on my bike. An appliance fails. I get a flat tire en route to an appointment. Someone I love is impatient and says something hurtful to me. Real life. In real life I am not a perfect model for Lao Tsu's four virtues. I get angry. I dodge telling the truth. I can be impatient and unfriendly. And there are even times when I become so self-absorbed with my own agenda that it becomes the only thing I pay attention to. It feels awful to admit this. On the other hand, I am not perfect. I try to not judge myself too harshly.

Of course, we all would prefer to have unassailable character expressed all day, every day. And I am confident that there are precious people alive who come very close to this ideal. I am not one of them. What keeps me going is that I am much closer than I once was. I would prefer to be perfect, but as long as there is progress and my course is set in the correct direction, I forgive myself over and over again.

For some readers, I know forgiving yourself and accepting failures is difficult.

Self-condemnation is unfortunately commonplace. I wonder if you could forgive me for my shortcomings? I make mistakes everyday. As long as I am genuinely engaged in the world and relating to other people, there is always something I can improve upon. Can you see my heart, my good intentions, even if my efforts fall short? Will you forgive me?… Thank you. I knew you would. Can you not forgive yourself similarly?

Sharon Salzberg, a brilliant meditation teacher, famously said, "You yourself, as much as anybody in the entire universe, deserve your love and affection." I love this quotation. It's so true and yet so often overlooked. No one can really walk in the world with a loving and kind character if they don't FIRST extend love and kindness to themselves. This is step one in cultivating a quality character. Perhaps you could put your hand over your heart right now. Breathe in and softly tell yourself that you will always take care of yourself. Tenderly say, "I love you" to yourself. And with genuine care and concern, repeat Salzberg's words, but make it personal: "As much as anybody in the entire universe, I deserve my love and affection." Believe it. If this short exercise is difficult for you, I urge you to make this affirmation practice a daily ritual. Tell yourself every day how special you are. You are worthy of your love and affection. You are a good person.

I ask this for you on behalf of me and all the beings in the universe. Your love for others will always be muted if you do not fully love and accept yourself. And when you do love and accept yourself, the resources you can give to others grow by leaps and bounds.

Your love for others will always be muted if you do not fully love and accept yourself.

I have tried to shoot pretty straight so far in this book. I have shared ideas that are either supported by science or they make a lot of common sense or both. Will you allow me to stretch a bit now?

In both western and eastern traditions there are mainstream notions of getting back what you give. I believe this entirely. In the Christian tradition there is a famous quote from Galatians: "A man reaps what he sows." That which a person puts into the world—thoughts, speech and deeds—comes back to that person with energetically identical returns. In the eastern traditions, there is a belief in Karma—it's a readily accessible concept related to cause and effect. Good actions result in good effects. Bad actions result in bad effects.

How could it really be any other way? YouTube has a popular series of videos with "instant karma" in the title. A typical vignette might look like this: A mean-spirited person lines up to kick a soccer ball at an unsuspecting person whose back is turned. The assailant kicks the ball with as much force as he can muster. He misses the intended victim and the ball rebounds off a fence post directly into his own face. Comical? Yes. Justice? For sure. How life works ordinarily? Rarely. We witness injustices frequently that go unpunished. And we see kind-hearted good deeds often go unnoticed and unrewarded.

Here's the stretch. I take it on faith that eventually our actions come back to be reflected in the quality of our own lives. Eastern religions generally hold that this karmic justice takes place over many lifetimes. I am uncertain about that, but I feel the laws of cause and effect in my own life. When I am in high spirits, friendly and positive, the world is generous to me. When I am kind and helpful to others, the universe is generally kind and helpful to me. And when cause and effect don't line up in ways that are transparent to me, I'm okay with that too. I know I will get my due, good and bad, eventually.

Your desire to cultivate a quality character is for your own reward. It's a happy coincidence that people and the environment also benefit from your efforts to be a good person.

Be good for your own sake. You deserve it.

Points to ponder:

- What are your top virtues? Create a list of virtues you embody regularly.
- What practices would help you be more attuned to the quality character you want to cultivate?

21 Summary

I read about an interesting social experiment not long ago. Harvard psychologist and researcher Dr. Ellen Langer wanted to know how to influence behavior change in others. They had two groups of randomly selected room cleaners from a large hotel. They examined each woman in each group for general health—blood pressure, body mass index, etc. They gave the women in one group a detailed lesson in healthy living. They learned all about diet and exercise. They were encouraged to make changes in their lives based on factual information that was shared with them. With the second group of women, the researchers explained in detail how much exercise each aspect of their cleaning work entailed. For example, they were told how many calories are burned vacuuming. Heart rates rise to "this level" when wiping down bathrooms. An average work day consists of "this" much vacuuming and "that" much wiping, resulting in cardiovascular effort of "this" and total calorie burn of "that". These maids got no healthy living education. Instead, they were given a lesson about the substantial physical demand that was present in their ordinary work lives.

A number of weeks later, the two groups of women were again examined for individual measures of health. Can you guess which group made the most improvement in terms of objective measures of health? It was NOT the one that was given excellent factual instruction about healthy exercise and diet. Instead, it was the women who were simply shown that they already had some essential aspects of healthy living built into each and every day at work. Why did these women then excel in terms of health outcomes? Why did they lose weight? Why did their blood pressure go down? They denied changing their lifestyle, whereas some of the women from the first group told researchers that they were implementing what they learned from the healthy living lessons.

What is going on with these unusual outcomes? Why is the one group of women getting healthier when they were not specifically educated about living a more healthy lifestyle?

The room cleaners who came to understand their existing lifestyles as being physically demanding understood themselves differently. Those who saw themselves as already very active, as responsible for, and as powerful in their own current practices—that is, getting lots of exercise each work day—knew themselves differently than they had before. By being educated about the challenge and demands of their physical labor, they saw themselves as people who already owned healthy lifestyles. This shaped their identity. More than the first group of room cleaners, these women saw themselves as healthy. We can guess that once they saw themselves as healthy, then other small and incremental changes started to shift for them. Since they now saw themselves as healthy people, they began behaving accordingly in other parts of their lives. Not only did they get a great workout from their jobs five days a week, they also did other things to benefit their health. Dr. Langer speculated that the women began making changes in their lives that were consistent with how they now saw themselves. Maybe they purchased and ate more fruit and vegetables—consistent with their self-image as healthy people. Maybe they walked, played sports, or otherwise engaged in some activities that other "healthy" people engage in. These shifts in behaviors were not pronounced for this group of women. It was subtle because these women were simply living in accord with their identity.

What's your identity? Are you someone who is committed to making gradual improvements in your life? You are; otherwise you wouldn't be reading this book. Are you someone who already has significant successes in your life? List them right here, right now! Where are you in terms of your general health? Are you doing some things (even one) to deliberately improve your nutrition, amount of exercise, or ability to rest and restore calm? What activity do you engage in that's mentally stimulating? With whom do you socialize? And in what ways is this company enriching your life? How do you connect to the larger world, the universe?

Write down every good thing you are doing to make your life better. I have done this exercise in workshop settings and it always motivates everyone in the room. Be grateful for where you are now. It's from this place that you will grow to a better, happier, healthier you!

Believe this. It's your identity. You are beautiful, healthy, happy and connected to everyone and everything. You already know it and are engaged in this growth in a number of areas in your life. The more clearly you can see this, the more readily you will progress toward your envisioned future self.

Just like the room cleaners, who know their true identity is one that includes healthy physical exercise, you are someone with a positive identity. Build on this. Believe it! See your goodness in your current place. If you haven't written down a list of attributes of your current activity, as described three paragraphs ago, do it now before reading on.

Your current activity and mindset are your identity, which can be used as a springboard to your future self. How will you be different one month from now? How will you build on your current identity to become who you most want to be one year from now? Five years from now? In your final happy years of old age?

Your current activity and mindset are your identity, which can be used as a springboard to your future self.

I recommend you write a detailed letter to yourself describing the various aspects of body, mind and spirit you will embody in the future—one month, one year, five years and in your final years of old age. Write this letter tenderly, as a promise to a most special loved one—you. Take your time to write this with all the care and attention you deserve, but start writing this letter straightaway. By doing so you are clarifying your identity. And just like the room cleaners, when you see this identity clearly you will begin to act into it effortlessly.

You Are Not Alone

We live in a pretty cynical culture. Mainstream media, in particular, is cynical. We are bombarded with bad news: terrorists, new diseases, corrupt politicians, etc. Celebrities are often shown at their worst: as cheaters, drunks and pompous spoiled brats. Often, it feels like things are getting worse. We hear that crime is out of control, violent deaths are rampant, obesity is an epidemic, and the planet is on a knife's edge of unsustainability. While we need to acknowledge that problems exist in our world, we also need to recognize that things are changing for the better,

In his book, *The Better Angels of Our Nature*, Stephen Pinker factually demonstrates that many qualities of human existence have never been better. Murder is down, as are deaths from war. More people than ever live with the basic right to democracy and the typical freedoms found therein. And, although there is still a long way to go, tolerance and equality is increasing for minority groups. An evolution of humanity is actively underway. Increasing levels of education, abundant global trade and international institutions, though imperfect, provide measures of order, safety and common ground for understanding.

How can these facts be true in light of mainstream culture shouting the opposite? They are true because many people just like you have been making choices to co-create a better world. Over time, people have moved to better government systems, created freedoms and democracies. People have made rules for commerce that often encourage a level of fairness. Individuals have studied and researched biology and medicine resulting in healthier and longer lives for everyone. People are choosing healthier foods such that entire stores dedicate themselves to meeting this need. Individuals are pursuing exercise and fitness as never before. Spiritual expression comes in many forms and these expressions have more commonalities than differences. People are marching for social justice and praying for peace. Individuals are meditating for their own calm and for the world's betterment. And many people, just like you, are reading this book and others like it in order to be happier. Individual choices to enhance well-being are the collective momentum.

My older son recently lamented how discouraging the drug culture is amongst his teenage peers. He felt alone in the moment, as though the tide of negative behaviors he sees is overwhelming. So we talked about what else he sees: his own healthy living and that of his closest friends and family. We considered some statistics that showed, generally, a decline in teenage drug usage, unwanted pregnancies and teenage violent crime. He is not alone in spite of the feelings he, and society as a whole, sometimes has.

The world is choosing a more balanced, healthier lifestyle. Creative beings are consciously making millions of individual choices that, collectively, are in the process of evolving the way we exist as a species. Together, we are powerful and we are in a process of making our own future. We are co-creating a future for humanity that is happier and intentionally leaning toward healthier, more balanced lives. Your efforts to create your best body, mind and spirit are the future for us all. Your success benefits everyone. And you are part of a massive swell of human consciousness toward this end. You are far from alone on the road to your best self. Moreover, the path you are on is a gift to the world.

Self-help—personal development—is sometimes portrayed by mainstream media as a self-absorbed hobby of a spoiled middle class. In some instances, it can be just that. But overall, one's personal effort to be their best self cannot be anything other than good for us all. To reflect on who we are and where we want to go is to consciously decide how to live. The worst of humanity is the unexamined/unconscious living that so many people do. You are different. You are a difference-maker—first in your own life and then, invariably, your experience and choices make wider and wider ripples across the ocean of humanity. It's never selfish to love and treat yourself well. Loving the world starts with loving yourself.

Thank you for sharing the journey of these written pages with me. I am grateful for the goodness in your heart that got you all the way to the end. Together, we are on an exciting ride called life. We have intersected here in this book. It would be a pleasure and an honor to connect elsewhere. Check out my website, perhaps send me an email, but above all else, be happy!

Paul Krismer

www.HappinessExperts.ca

Afterword

People ask me if I am always happy. I suppose this happens because I call myself a "Happiness Expert" and because, when I am giving presentations, I am doing what I love to do: teaching holistic happiness. Of course, I have moments of unhappiness in my life. I have suffered painful losses. I worry and ruminate about things that are often out of my control. And still, after all these years of knowing better, I seek the approval of others so I can feel good about myself.

I suppose all those foibles make me pretty normal. I do, however, know with utter certainty, that the trajectory of my life propels me toward more meaning, greater contentment and better resilience against life's trials. I'm generally a pretty happy guy. For this, I owe a tremendous debt of gratitude to the many sources of inspiration for how I think about and live my life.

In this book, I have referenced other people's work, from which I have shared specific expertise. Much more often, no scholar is given credit for the ideas I have shared. This is not because I have shared original thoughts borne of my own creative juices. Rather, it's because I have amalgamated many people's ideas over a great many years. I have forgotten more sources of inspiration than I have remembered. An apology is in order to all the men and women whose influence has found some expression on these pages. I am sorry for not referencing your contribution. I am sincerely grateful for the ideas that have influenced me and I hope your ideas, through my words, will favorably influence others.

It's fair to say a "good life" isn't as complicated as the thousands of words preceding this paragraph may suggest. Simplicity is, itself, beautiful and that which is said simply is often much more true than any long-winded exposition. So I say this:

Happiness eludes those who chase it, but voluntarily accompanies those who worry little about its acquisition.

Live ethically. To be well is to know you have been fair and upright.

Treat yourself as your most treasured friend. You owe this to yourself.

Assume you can get where you want to go, then walk into your intentions.

Fear and doubt are just emotions. They will be sure to come and go. When they arise, carry on living into your intentions.

The happy feeling we have when we share the company of a good friend is founded on your warmth and kindness. Be warm and kind and you will have a good life.

Visit me at www.HappinessExperts.ca and let me know what your recipe for the good life is. I would love to hear from you.

Paul Krismer
November 17, 2016

Acknowledgements

Special acknowledgement is necessary here.

My editor, Carmel Ecker, is not only exceptionally good at what she does, she is also one of the kindest, best friends I could ever ask for. Thank you, Carmel. This book, for all its weaknesses, is infinitely better due to your careful, brilliant review.

Also, a shout out to Becky Norwood is warranted. Her skills and experience took this project from dream to reality. Thank you Becky!

Made in the USA
Monee, IL
29 August 2020